T3-BUU-850

As the Spirit Moves

As the Spirit Moves

Edited with Commentary by

Nancy D. Potts, Ed.D.

Peace Publishing
Austin, Texas

FRONT COVER DESIGN AND ILLUSTRATIONS
BY EDWARD ISAAC PAUL BURKLE
BACK COVER DESIGN BY LaVONNE PROSSER
COVER LOGO BY SANDIE ZILKER

As the Spirit Moves. Copyright © 1994 by Nancy D. Potts. All rights reserved. Printed in the United States of America. No part of this book may be reproduced in any form or by any means, electronic or mechanical, including photocopying, recording, taping, or any retrieval system, without the written permission of Peace Publishing, 303 Camp Craft Rd., Suite 250, Austin, Texas 78746.

98   97   96   95   94   5   4   3   2   1

Library of Congress Cataloging-in-Publication Data

Potts, Nancy D.
  As the Spirit Moves/Nancy D. Potts-1st ed.
  Includes bibliographical references and illustrations.
  ISBN 0-9640010-2-0   CIP 94-067967
  1. Spirituality.   2. Inspirational.   3. Literature.

Printed by Morgan Printing & Publishing, Inc., Austin, Texas 78756

For additional copies, write:
Peace Publishing
303 Camp Craft Rd., Suite 250
Austin, Texas 78746

To Master Storytellers,
East and West,
whose illumined lives mark the quest
to God for others who follow in their footsteps,
and
To those at The Peace Institute
of Universal Christianity,
whose selfless work helped to make
this book possible.

CONTENTS

ILLUSTRATIONS

Acknowledgments

Stories act as a wayshower to the Divine, drawing people of every culture and tradition from our limited mortal consciousness into God Consciousness. The deep, sublime stories of the spiritual quest spark our imagination and zero in on the heart of our nature. We discover in traditions East and West that our vocation in this life is, through self-effort, to embrace fully the soul's journey to union with God in love. Stories of the quest are a bridge of hope over a chasm of endless desires, a footpath which supports us on our journey Home.

We are grateful beyond measure for this bridge and for the teachers of wisdom, past and present, who have selflessly shared with us the landmarks of the quest, the disciplines of realization, and the stories which silently draw us inside the temple of God that resides in our own hearts.

In the spirit of compassionate service, those at The Peace Institute of Universal Christianity have offered a treasury of talent to help bring this garden of stories into full bloom. Thank you, one and all, for your tireless and committed work on *As the Spirit Moves.*

To Marilyn Hamor, a knowledgeable reader and supportive friend, my deep appreciation for her unfailing inspiration and for nurturing the garden of stories with her grace, humor, wisdom, and editorial comments.

To Ann Mellor, my deep and lasting gratitude for creating a coherent architecture for the garden through her skilled computer work and management of endless details, revisions, proofing and deadline schedules. With humor, dedication, and selfless discipline, she worked with both the thorns and flowers of the garden, day and night, on work days and vacation days.

To Shirlene Bridgewater, my deep gratitude for her professional editing skills, commitment to literary accuracy, and for long days of creative work at The Peace Institute. Thank you for gently removing the weeds to enhance the natural flowering of the garden.

To Janet Leubner, my deep appreciation for the marketing expertise and love with which the garden of stories is provided to those whose hearts are prepared to receive unfolding flowers of the spirit. Thank you for your patience with questions, revisions, and "flexibility drills" of a new self-publishing project.

To Janet Lake, my gratitude for long hours of computer work and efficient administrative support in the office and on behalf of this book. Without her care for the roots of the garden—author permission requests—there would be no stories to reprint.

To Mary Jane Lamonte, my appreciation for generous help in the final preparation of the manuscript and skilled attention to the reference material. Always willing to help where needed, she cared for the details of the garden with a skilled literary eye.

To Lanette Buehler, who watered and pruned flowers of the garden with a dedicated heart, and to Alyse Kyriay who helped in often unheralded but essential ways, my heartfelt gratitude.

To the talented volunteers who so generously gave their time and expertise, my special thanks for the humor and dedication with which they traced down missing quotation marks, wandering participles, and sentences which jumped beyond the margins of the garden. These trusted proofreaders know the garden by heart; to each of you, thank you: Sharon Bradford, Amanda Buehler, Lanette Buehler, Bethany Cunha, Marilyn Hamor, Alyse Kyriay, Janet Lake, Mary Jane Lamonte, Janet Leubner, Karin Runciman, Suzanne Smith, and Trish Taylor.

To LaVonne Prosser and Sandie Zilker, my deep gratitude for such a beautifully designed back cover and logo that has become our standard "home" for written texts; and to Ann Mellor and Shirlene Bridgewater, who wrote and edited the words that grace the back cover, my heartfelt thanks.

To Edward Isaac Paul "Buck" Burkle, my heartfelt gratitude for the beautiful front cover design and layout and for his book illustrations, each designed to evoke the universal wisdom of the quest. With sensitivity and a dedicated spirit, he created gentle images of grace and beauty which flower in the heart.

To the Friends of The Peace Institute whose generous financial contributions have made this book possible, my everlasting gratitude.

To Morgan Printing's Buck Burkle, Mike Morgan, Terry Sherrell, and Dawn McGehee, grateful acknowledgment for the important assistance, advice, and guidance we received on each phase of this project.

Now the garden of stories is ready. Weeds have been pulled; the flowers watered and pruned. Long, slender roots have stretched their arms into the black earth while new-born leaves drink from the light of the sun.

The collaboration of the gardeners was a gift to those who realize that within the walls of our worldly activities exists a secret garden of the heart. The door is now open to the color-splashed landscape of our own being. Enter with reverence and a sense of wonder.

Lord make me an instrument of thy Peace;
Where there is hatred, let me sow Love;
Where there is injury, Pardon;
Where there is doubt, Faith;
Where there is despair, Hope;
Where there is sadness, Joy;
Where there is darkness, Light;
O Divine Master,
Grant that I may not seek to be consoled, as to console,
To be understood, as to understand,
To be loved, as to love;
For it is in giving that we receive,
It is in pardoning that we are pardoned,
It is in dying that we are born to Eternal Life.

Saint Francis of Assisi

Introduction

The universe is made up of stories. They nourish, awaken, inspire, teach. Great Masters of every tradition used stories as a bridge to connect us to patterns, possibilities, and rhythms of the universe. The teaching stories of Jesus, for example, taught us about love, compassion, courage, forgiveness, and wisdom. His stories were like a light shining into darkness, revealing the possibility of transformation.

Every worthwhile journey requires that we enter unfamiliar territory. This is especially true in the spiritual life where we learn what is most profound in the depths of unknown realms. The growth, awakenings, hindrances, dark nights, and death-rebirth experiences of the spiritual journey are the stories of the spirit passed on from teacher to student, from ancient times to today. They open our heart to the sacred and a new way of being.

As the spirit moves through stories of the spiritual quest, we make fundamental discoveries about the spiritual life. We realize that fulfillment lies not in what we receive, but in our growing ability to give of ourselves. We learn to speak with compassion, serve the good of the whole, offer kindness and respect. As we come together to serve a higher purpose, we give up old fears, limitations, and barriers. Healing occurs as we allow ourselves to awaken to our original goodness as children of God.

We also discover that there comes a time when maps and directions from spiritual books cannot prepare us for the unknown or provide that depth necessary to travel beyond our own self. Friendly guidance and support from another on the spiritual path can assist us. In an environment of trust and compassion, the heart opens into a beautiful blossom of the spirit. Old parts of us die; new ones are born in a protected, sacred space. In the process, we learn to love truth, trust ourselves, give and receive love. It is a gift of love without conditions in which we are invited to be open to the sacred within us.

Inspired by people who live and teach peace in the midst of worldly turmoil, we look at our own lives and at our own inner revelations of harmony,

1

when judgment drops away and compassion emerges. We discover that each person in front of us is ourselves in disguise, yearning for love and forgiveness; that to judge another is to disconnect from our own pain and sorrow, to withdraw from our own hearts. As judgment is transformed into love and compassion, however, we see the interconnectedness of us all and reach greater depths of tolerance, humility, and forgiveness. Love and wisdom become part of our own unfolding story as a pilgrim along the Way.

As we are moved by stories of the quest, we discover that the act of living in peace is a journey of transformation. It requires great love, discipline, compassion, humor, courage, and a willingness to face that which hides in the shadows of consciousness. By turning to face hidden aspects of our lives, we cast away fear, doubt, and limitations. Difficulties, met without judgment and prejudice, become transforming. Challenges become opportunities to develop greater depths of wisdom and compassion. Peace becomes an open heart which embraces all aspects of our lives, and we enter peaceful cooperation with body, mind, family, neighbors, culture, the earth, God. No longer lost in our reactions, we live in a conscious harmony of thoughts, words, and actions. We live in peace; we become peace; we are peace.

This book is a collection of stories, parables, and sacred scriptures, drawn from many cultures and centuries, from great traditions East and West, both ancient and contemporary. Each story—Christian, Buddhist, Hindu, Sufi, Zen, Chinese, Hassidic, Russian, Native American, African, Chassid, and other sources—is alive with the inspiration and wisdom of its tradition. Each story can teach us that love, forgiveness, courage, and transformation can be part of our own unfolding story; and, if read in a certain way, each story can produce spiritual growth.

The stories in *As the Spirit Moves* are divided into three sections, each highlighting an aspect or phase of the spiritual journey. Part I, "The Quest," awakens us to the greatest adventure of them all, the spiritual quest to our true nature wherein is revealed our divine heritage and destiny. Part II, "Lighting the Divine Fire," describes the hills and valleys of the spiritual journey and the disciplines of realization which intensify our longing to follow the "trail of light." The stories in these chapters speak to simplicity, obstacles, faith, attachments, prayer and meditation, love, forgiveness, humility, service, and the integrity and compassion which accompany awakening. In Part III, "Ascent of the Mountain of Truth," we scale the highest reaches of consciousness to the heart of existence. In a passage through consciousness to our deepest center, we unmask all that is not God to ultimately live in full unity with the Divine. In stories of illumination, glimpses of unity, and the symbolic caterpillar/cocoon/butterfly stages of spiritual unfoldment, we discover that the more light of understanding we have, the more we become aware of our spiritual immaturity until we are immersed in a sea of light in absolute unknowing. Then the heart, full of love, is a cascading river overflowing its banks to embrace all in its path. Spiritual transformation is an alchemical process that changes ignorance into an embodiment of love, wisdom, integrity, and compassion.

The spiritual quest to our highest potential awakens the heart to that which is beyond knowledge, beyond words and concepts. The priceless gift of stories can inspire us to listen, be silent, contemplate; to think, reflect, talk less and be more receptive to the spirit behind the story. As we do so, we see all things with a different eye. Our heart is full of wonder. Deep contemplation produces wonder, not withdrawal; attention and absorption, not indifference. Contemplation arises when we are fully in the present moment without thoughts of the past or images of the future. We glimpse God in such timeless moments. Stories of the quest, if read properly, can lead us into the place where the heart sings.

In receptive silence, listen to the message of each story, take it inside, let it merge with the rhythm of your heart and life. Experience the humor and poignancy, the poetry and music, the images and delight in stories of Truth. Like a raft which carries us between two shores, tales of the quest take us across the sea, into the heartland of our own being.

How do we read stories of the spirit? There are many ways to kneel and kiss the ground, many paths up the mountain of Truth. But there are helpful pointers along the way. To read a story once is to receive entertainment. To read a story again in silent reflection is to touch its essence. To read it once again *after* reflection, creating a silent space within us for it to reveal its inner depth and meaning, is to allow the story to resonate at ever-new levels, giving us a feel for the mystical. To penetrate to the hidden depths of the story, carry it around all day, letting its melody become a haunting refrain.

Stories are seeds, full of life and energy, waiting to fall on fertile, receptive ground. May they grow in the garden of the soul and give us understanding, courage, and hope. In return, may we welcome each story, every moment with a compassionate heart. May we bow in reverent respect to the spirit within all that lives—our sisters and brothers, the sun and stars, the trees and flowers, the birds of the sky and the rocks of the earth. This is the story of *As the Spirit Moves*.

Nancy D. Potts
Austin, Texas
August 1994

Part I

The Quest

The Quest

There is another kind of exploration than that which traverses deserts, penetrates jungles, climbs mountains, and crosses continents. It seeks out the mysterious hinterlands of the human mind, scales the highest reaches of human consciousness, and then returns to report routes and discoveries, describe the goals to others so that they also may find their way thereto if they wish.

Paul Brunton

As we awaken from the sleep of life, we embark on a Homeward journey that begins and ends with the heart. It is the *quest*. It is not, however, a journey of miles or days. It is not a quest for pleasure, comfort, fame, or power. It is a *spiritual* quest, a conscious dedication to search for Truth in our deepest center of consciousness. This ageless journey is the greatest adventure of them all. It is, quite simply, the Great Work, the Universal Mystery for which all of our life on Earth is a preparation.

In every period of history, in all world cultures, we discover tales of this heroic quest hidden in stories, poems, myths, songs, dreams, and literature which perpetuate the esoteric doctrines of spiritual rebirth. Like a river singing its way to its Source, these chronicles of the inner life record the song of the heart and its message of hope and joy, death and rebirth, wisdom and compassion. But, until we embark on this extraordinary journey of the human spirit, the singing brook is silent to us, the inner mysteries hidden. We live in a blanket of mist that veils the heart's deepest mysteries until the dawn of our awakening. When we seek our own true nature, however, we have begun the quest.

We begin with the chapter *Awakening* in which we discover stories of love, faith, wisdom, and courage. Stories open the flower of the heart and inspire us to look beyond what we can see, hear, and touch; to appreciate the enormous strength and love within us; to be profoundly moved by the joys and sorrows of the human experience. Each of us has the capacity for love and forgiveness, reverence and faith, integrity and compassion. To awaken to the sacred is to honor the potential within us. Therefore, our first responsibility is to become conscious of our true nature and seek the highest welfare of our inner Self.

Awakening invites us to look with new eyes at our own life. What are we cultivating in the garden of our soul—faith, hope, the spirit of reverence or criticism, judgment, rewards for service and love? What turmoil in our lives could be healed by forgiveness and compassion? What unrealized dreams hide in the silence of our soul?

In *The Pilgrimage*, we discover that, whether we scale a mountain or awaken the Spirit, it calls for interior footwork, a prayer of the feet. By its nature a pilgrimage requires that we enter unfamiliar territory, with reverence and faith, to walk in the shadows of an unknown region. We abandon the ship of security to listen to what we cannot hear and see what we cannot envision. Wakeful to the Spirit, we seek that unseen treasure hidden in the heart of existence.

But it is not a journey for the timid. Everyone's history is written in the soul awaiting our discovery. The courageous pilgrim who charts a course through unknown realms must draw on the inner resources of dedication, perseverance, and steadfastness. Occasional detours may be accompanied by the inevitable fear that we have lost our way, and we may flounder in doubts and uncertainties as we enter the gates of illusion. But each difficulty becomes an opportunity to embrace Truth amid the storms of consciousness, to find peace amid turmoil. *Challenge is only an opportunity for growth in disguise.* As we gently accept all that comes our way, we move beyond the concerns of win/ lose, gain/loss, pleasure/pain. Inner trust deepens; no longer can we lie down under the blanket of ignorance. The silence of the night is now a dream of eternity. The heart, now a temple, sings a hymn of thanksgiving. Pilgrimage is homecoming and the discovery that what we have sought "had been living unseen next to [us] all the time."

The Pilgrimage can inspire us to look at our own unique journey. What are our current obstacles and struggles, and can we open our hearts to accept the opportunities in disguise? Are we willing to allow challenges to open us to greater depths of wisdom and compassion?

In *Who Am I?*, we discover that the sleeping hero within us is our Real Self awaiting resurrection. Our journey through the sea of consciousness brings us to the shore of our own being, where the mystery of our true nature is revealed in all its majestic splendor. Before the revelation of the "kingdom of heaven," however, Truth remains hidden, known in its effects, but not yet as an *experiential* mystery.

It is our spiritual destiny to know who we are in our deepest center. As a ship returns to port empty but joyous, we, too, return to our home harbor welcomed by morning light. But when we gaze into scenes of our scattered personal world, we see long shadows of night stretching over the surface of our consciousness. Our lives may be filled with the darkness of loss, rejection, pain, and vulnerability—the hallmarks of life's common experiences. We may be tempted to put aside our search for Truth; our own vulnerability may leave us afraid, giving rise to feelings of anger, blame, or hostility.

The art of living is to discover our true nature of light amid darkness. Rather than fleeing shadows, we turn toward what is everlasting within us. To deny what haunts our inner life can create untold suffering; to gracefully and gently accept what lurks in the shadows can be transforming. As Saint John of the Cross said, "If a person wishes to be sure of the road they tread upon, they must close their eyes and walk in the dark."

Walk in the dark. Discover our true nature amid the shadows of life. Greatness of spirit, love, compassion, and faith reside in all of us, awaiting our discovery.

As we read the stories in this section, reflect on the light amid darkness. What do we resist in the shadows? How can we discover the wisdom and love of our true nature? How can we embrace what lies in the shadows and allow it to become our teacher of compassion?

Chapter I

The Awakening

When Life Was Full There Was No History

In the age when life on earth was full, no one paid any special attention to worthy men, nor did they single out the man of ability. Rulers were simply the highest branches on the trees and the people were like deer in the woods. They were honest and righteous without realizing that they were "doing their duty." They loved each other and did not know this was "love of neighbor." They deceived no one yet did not know they were "men to be trusted." They were reliable and did not know that this was "good faith." They lived freely together giving and taking and did not know they were generous. For this reason their deeds have not been narrated. They made no history.

Chuang Tzu

We Understand So Little

Once there were two young brothers who had spent all their lives in the city and had never even seen a field or pasture. So one day they decided to take a trip into the countryside. As they were walking along, they spied a farmer plowing and were puzzled about what he was doing.

"What kind of behavior is this?" they asked themselves. "This fellow marches back and forth all day, scarring the earth with long ditches. Why should anyone destroy such a pretty meadow like that?"

Later in the afternoon they passed the same place again, and this time they saw the farmer sowing grains of wheat in the furrows.

"Now what's he doing?" they asked themselves. "He must be a madman. He's taking perfectly good wheat and tossing it into these ditches!"

"The country is no place for me," said one of the brothers. "The people here act as if they had no sense. I'm going home." And he went back to the city.

But the second brother stayed in the country, and a few weeks later saw a wonderful change. Fresh green shoots began to cover the field with a lushness he had never imagined. He quickly wrote to his brother and told him to hurry back to see the miraculous growth.

So his brother returned from the city, and he, too, was amazed at the change. As the days passed they saw the green earth turn into a golden field of tall wheat. And now they understood the reason for the farmer's work.

Then the wheat grew ripe, and the farmer came with his scythe and began to cut it down. The brother who had returned from the city couldn't believe it. "What is this imbecile doing now?" he exclaimed. "All summer long he worked so hard to grow this beautiful wheat, and now he's destroying it with his own hands! He is a madman after all! I've had enough. I'm going back to the city."

But his brother had more patience. He stayed in the country and watched the farmer collect the wheat and take it to his granary. He saw how cleverly he separated the chaff, and how carefully he stored the rest. And he was filled with awe when he realized that by sowing a bag of seed, the farmer had harvested a whole field of grain. Only then did he truly understand that the farmer had a reason for everything he did.

"And this is how it is with God's works, too," he said. "We mortals see only the beginnings of His plan. We cannot understand the full purpose and end of His creation. So we must have faith in His wisdom."

Jewish Folktale

Buddha pictures lack of knowledge this way: it is as if you are clinging to the branch of a tree in the thick darkness of night, so that you cannot see what is beneath you, whether it is land or sea. Then you are always afraid of falling. You keep on clinging to the tree, and, yet, you are suffering with the fear of how long it will be before you have to let go. How long can you cling to the branch? Yet under your feet there is nothing! Such is life until light comes. Then it is like the coming of the sun. When the sun rises, you find there is no water, for the land is just beneath your feet.

Buddhist

Often when a person is quite unprepared for such a thing, and is not even thinking of God, he is awakened by His Majesty, as though by a rushing comet or a thunderclap. Although no sound is heard, the soul is very well aware that it has been called by God.

Saint Teresa of Ávila

❧❧❧❧❧❧❧

Towards the end of the 1950s, the various negative aspects of my life had made me into a neurotic, incapable of loving, inhibited, apprehensive and with a gloomy cast of mind which sometimes impelled me to long for death as the only way out of an unendurable existence . . . .

At this time, my husband and I met the man who was to become the dearest friend of both of us. For me it was the closest relationship of mind and spirit, frequently telepathic, that I have ever known or expect to know: one which I could never have dared to hope for or believe possible.

[Then] he died suddenly. One had known that his life would not be long, as his health had always been wretched, but, nevertheless, the shock and desolation were crushing. I remember thinking: 'At a time like this, a belief in the soul's immortality must be the most tremendous support.' But I could not pretend to share it, and indeed did not try to.

On the following Sunday my husband and I were driving along a country road . . . . We were talking sorrowfully of our dear friend, when suddenly I knew that his spirit lived and was as close to me that moment as it had ever been in life. When I say I knew, words are inadequate to convey the experience. This was 'knowing' more vivid and real than anything I have ever experienced in the literal sense. It was as if for a moment one had known reality and in comparison the world of the senses was the dream. I was filled with an unutterable joy, which I shall never be able to describe. I seemed to apprehend, in a measure, the inexhaustible love of God for us, which envelops the universe and everything in it. Above all, I understood beyond all questioning that nothing in life, however seemingly insignificant, is ever lost or purposeless, but all tends towards the fulfillment of a design which one day will be made clear to us . . . .

From the day of what I can only consider my rebirth my neurotic difficulties disappeared and have never since returned.

Meg Maxwell and Verena Tschudin, *Seeing the Invisible*
from the Alister Hardy Research Center

❧❧❧❧❧❧❧

Simply to speak of the laws of nature is enough to arouse deep admiration. But when they are fully understood, they are as fields full of flowers, whose lavish blossoms give out a spiritual sweetness like nectar from heaven.

Philokalia 3:61

What is life? It is the flash of a firefly in the night. It is the breath of a buffalo in the winter time. It is the little shadow which runs across the grass and loses itself in the Sunset.

Crowfoot

At seventeen I was confused and questing. Nothing made a lot of sense; the world seemed so unfair and people unreliable. However, I had not forgotten how to pray; and I prayed with unashamed sincerity that if God existed, could He show me some sort of light in the jungle.

One day, I was sweeping the stairs down in the house in which I was working, when suddenly I was overcome, overwhelmed, saturated . . . with a sense of most sublime and living *love*. It not only affected me, but seemed to bring everything around me to *life*. The brush in my hand, my dustpan, the stairs, seemed to come alive with love. I seemed no longer me, with my petty troubles and trials, but part of this infinte power of love, so utterly and overwhelmingly wonderful that one knew at once what the saints had grasped. It could only have been a minute or two, yet for that brief particle of time it seemed eternity . . . .

Meg Maxwell and Verena Tschudin, *Seeing the Invisible*
from the Alister Hardy Research Center

A remarkable thing took place, worth wide remembrance, in the community of Gubbio. While Saint Francis was still alive, in the region thereabouts was a fearful wolf, enormous in size and most ferocious in the savagery of his hunger. It had devoured not only animals but men and women too, so much that it held all the people in such terror that they all went armed whenever they went into the countryside as if they were off to grim war. Even armed, they were not able to escape the tearing teeth and ravening rage of the wolf, if by mischance they met him. Such terror gripped them all that scarcely anyone dared to go outside the city gate.

It was God's will to emphasize for those townsfolk the holiness of Saint Francis, since the blessed father was at that very time among them. In pity for them he made arrangements to go out and meet the wolf. "Have care, Brother Francis, not to go outside the gate," they said, "because the wolf who has devoured many will surely kill you." But Saint Francis, hoping in the Lord Jesus Christ who rules the spirits of all flesh, without the protection of shield or helmet, but guarding himself with the Sign of the Holy Cross, went out of the gate with a companion, putting all his trust in the Lord who makes all who believe in him "walk without harm over viper and asp, but tread not only on the wolf, but on the lion too and the serpent." So the most faithful Francis went fearlessly out to meet the wolf. Many were watching from places they had climbed to see. That fearsome wolf rushed out against Saint Francis and his friend with open mouth. The blessed father met him with the Sign of the Cross, and by divine strength restrained the wolf from himself and his companion, checked its charge and closed its cruelly open mouth. Calling him then, he said: "Come to me, brother wolf, and in Christ's name I command you not to harm me or anybody." It is wondrous that one Sign of the Cross closed that awful maw. As soon as the order was given, like a lamb and not a wolf, with lowered head he laid himself at the feet of the saint. Saint Francis said to him: "Brother wolf, you wreak much harm in these parts and have done some dreadful deeds, destroying creatures of God without mercy. Not only brute beasts do you kill, but, a deed of more hateful boldness, you kill and devour men and women made in the image of God. So you deserve an awful death, to be hacked like any footpad or loathly murderer. That is why all justly cry out and murmur against you and the whole city is your foe. But, brother wolf, I want you and them to make peace so that they may be no more harmed by you, nor the hounds further pursue you."

The wolf showed by movements of his body, tail and ears and the bowing of its head, that he accepted without reservation what the saint said. Saint Francis continued: "Brother wolf, in view of your undertaking to make this peace, I promise you that as long as you live you will be given what you need by the people of this community, so that you will no more suffer hunger, for I know that whatever evil you do you do because of the ravening hunger. But, my brother wolf, since I secure such favor for you, I want you to promise me that you will never harm any animal or man. Do you so promise?" And the wolf by proper bowing of his head showed that he promised to keep the undertakings put to him by the saint. Saint Francis said: "Brother wolf, I want you to give me a pledge that I can confidently accept that you will keep your promise," and when Saint Francis held out his hand to receive the pledge, the wolf lifted his right front paw and softly and gently placed it in Saint Francis' hand, giving such pledge as he could. Then said Saint Francis: "Brother wolf, I bid you in the name of the Lord Jesus Christ to come along with me, without fear, into the city to make this peace in the name of Jesus Christ." The wolf immediately set off to go with the saint like the gentlest lamb.

Seeing this, the citizens were dumbfounded. The miracle echoed through the community so that men and women, great and small, congregated in the square where Saint Francis was with the wolf. The populace was there in a horde when Saint Francis rose and preached a wondrous sermon. It was, he said, because of their sins that such scourges were allowed; and how much more perilous was the flame of Gehenna's fire which can devour the damned forever, than the ravening of a wolf which can kill only the body; and how terrible it was to be plunged into the jaws of hell when one poor animal could hold so huge a crowd in panic and peril. "Return, therefore, dear friends, to the Lord and do proper penance, and God will free you from the wolf now, and in the future from the pit of consuming fire. Listen, dear folk, for brother wolf who is present here has promised me and pledged his word to make peace with you, to do no one harm if you promise to give him his daily necessities. And on his behalf I promise and pledge to you that he will faithfully observe the pact of peace." Then all there gathered with a mighty shout and promised to feed the wolf forever. And Saint Francis said to the wolf before them all: "And do you, brother wolf, promise to keep faith with them, and do harm to neither man nor beast." The wolf knelt and bowed his head, and with conciliatory movements of body, tail and ears, indicated that he would keep his promise.

Saint Francis said: "Brother wolf, just as you gave me your word outside the gate, here now before these people give me your word that you will not betray me." Then the wolf lifted his right paw and pledged himself with everyone standing round. All were lost in joy and wonder as much for the devotion of the saint as for the strangeness of the miracle, and they made the welkin ring acclaiming the peace of wolf and people, praising and blessing the Lord Jesus Christ who sent Saint Francis to them. By his merits he freed them from the fear of the loathly beast, and, out of so awful a visitation, restored to them peace and quiet.

Both kept the pact Saint Francis had arranged, and for two years the wolf went from door to door begging. Harming no one, and harmed by no one, he lived like a state ward. It was wonderful that no dog barked at him. At length he grew old and died, and the citizens mourned him, for by his peaceful and kind forbearance, he recalled to mind the worth and holiness of Saint Francis whenever he went through the town. To the praise and glory of the Lord Jesus Christ. Amen.

I claim to be an average man of less than average ability. I have not the shadow of a doubt that any man or woman can achieve what I have, if he or she would make the same effort and cultivate the same hope and faith.

Mahatma Gandhi

Great men are they who see that the spiritual is stronger than any material force and that thought rules the world.

Ralph Waldo Emerson

Although religion had meant a lot to me, at the same time I was going through a period of doubt and disillusion with life and was torn by conflict . . . . On this particular June day I had time to fill in. It was a glorious sunny evening and I walked through St. James's Park and sat down by the water intending to read. I never opened my book.

It was very beautiful, with the sun glinting through the trees and the ducks swimming on the water, and quite suddenly I felt lifted beyond all the turmoil and the conflict. There was no visual image and I knew I was sitting on a seat in the park, but I felt as if I was lifted above the world and looking down on it. The disillusion and cynicism were gone and I felt compassion suffusing my whole being, compassion for all people on earth. I was possessed by a peace that I have never felt before or since and—what is to me most interesting and curious of all—this whole state was not emotional; it was as if I was not without emotion but beyond it. The experience passed off gradually and I suppose it lasted twenty to thirty minutes.

At the time I felt it was an experience of God, because I interpreted it according to my own religious framework.

Meg Maxwell and Verena Tschudin, *Seeing the Invisible*
from The Alister Hardy Research Center

Abbot Anastasius had a book written on very fine parchment which was worth eighteen pence and had in it both the Old and New Testaments in full. Once a certain brother came to visit him, and, seeing the book, made off with it. So that day when Abbot Anastasius went to read his book, and found that it was gone, he realized that the brother had taken it. But he did not send after him to inquire about it for fear that the brother might add perjury to theft. Well, the brother went down into the nearby city in order to sell the book. And the price he asked was sixteen pence. The buyer said: Give me the book that I may find out whether it is worth that much. With that, the buyer took the book to the holy Anastasius and said: Father, take a look at this book, please, and tell me whether you think I ought to buy it for sixteen pence. Is it worth that much? Abbot Anastasius said: Yes, it is a fine book, it is worth that much. So the buyer went back to the brother and said: Here is your money. I showed the book to Abbot Anastasius, and he said it is a fine book and is worth at least sixteen pence. But the brother asked: Was that all he said? Did he make any other remarks? No, said the buyer, he did not say another word. Well, said the brother, I have changed my mind and I don't want to sell this book after all. Then he hastened to Abbot Anastasius and begged him with tears to take back his book, but the Abbot would not accept it, saying: Go in peace, brother, I make you a present of it. But the brother said: If you do not take it back I shall never have any peace. After that the brother dwelt with Abbot Anastasius for the rest of his life.

Desert Fathers

Once some robbers came into the monastery of the desert fathers and said to one of the elders: We have come to take away everything that is in your cell. And he said: My sons, take all you want. So they took everything they could find in the cell and started off. But they left behind a little bag that was hidden in the cell. The elder picked it up and followed after them, crying out: My sons, take this, you forgot it in the cell! Amazed at the patience of the elder, they brought everything back into his cell and did penance, saying: This one really is a man of God!

Desert Fathers

 za za za za za za za

A big, tough samurai once went to see a little monk. "Monk," he said, in a voice accustomed to instant obedience, "teach me about heaven and hell!"

The monk looked up at this mighty warrior and replied with utter disdain, "Teach you about heaven and hell? I couldn't teach you about anything. You're dirty. You smell. Your blade is rusty. You're a disgrace, an embarrassment to the samurai class. Get out of my sight. I can't stand you."

The samurai was furious. He shook, got all red in the face, was speechless with rage. He pulled out his sword and raised it above him, preparing to slay the monk.

"That's hell," said the monk softly.

The samurai was overwhelmed. The compassion and surrender of this little man who had offered his life to give this teaching to show him hell! He slowly put down his sword, filled with gratitude, and suddenly [became] peaceful.

"And that's heaven," said the monk softly.

Zen

za za za za za za za

One afternoon I was lying down resting after a long walk on the Plain . . . . The grass was hot and I was on an eye level with insects moving about. Everything was warm, busy and occupied with living. I was relaxed but extraneous to the scene.

Then it happened: a sensation of bliss. No loss of consciousness, but increased consciousness . . . I could feel the earth under me right down to the centre of the earth, and I belonged to it and it belonged to me. I also felt that the insects were my brothers and sisters, and all that was alive was related to me, because we were all living matter that died to make way for the next generation . . . . And I felt and experienced everything that existed, even sounds and colours and tastes, all at once, and it was all blissful . . . . I had a conviction that a most important truth had been enunciated: that we are all related—animal, vegetable and mineral—so no one is alone. I have never forgotten this experience.

Meg Maxwell and Verena Tschudin, *Seeing the Invisible*
from The Alister Hardy Research Center

ཙཔ ཙཔ ཙཔ ཙཔ ཙཔ

The Banyan Deer

Once, the Buddha was born as a Banyan Deer. When he was grown he became leader of the herd. He guided his herd wisely and led them to the heart of a secluded forest where, sheltered by the giant trees, they lived free from danger.

Then a new king came into power over the land. And, above all things, this king loved hunting. As soon as the sun rose, he would mount his horse and lead his men on a furious chase through fields and meadows, forests, and glens. Shooting his arrows madly, he would not leave off until the sun had set. Then the wagons rolled back to the palace behind him, filled now with deer, boar, rabbit, pheasant, monkey, leopard, bear, tiger, and lion. And the king was happy.

His people, however, were not pleased. Fields had been ruined by the royal hunt. Farmers and merchants had been forced to leave off their work in order to beat the jungles and drive the hidden beasts towards the waiting king and his men. Affairs of state, too, lay unattended.

The people, determined to bring all this to an end, devised a simple plan. They built a stockade deep in the forest. "We'll trap a herd or two of deer in this stockade," they said. "Then the king can hunt all he wants. Let him hunt to his heart's content. He won't ruin our fields or force us to leave our shops. Then let him be happy."

The stockade was built and two herds of deer were driven within its walls. The gates were closed and the delicate animals, charging and wheeling in frantic circles, sought some way out. But there was none. Exhausted at last, they stood trembling, awaiting their fate.

The men left happily to tell the king of their success.

One of the herds that had been captured was the herd of the Banyan Deer.

The Banyan Deer walked among his herd. Sunlight played on his many-branched antlers. His black eyes shone and his muzzle was wet. "The blue sky is overhead. Green grass grows at our feet," he told the others. "Do not give up. Where there is life, there is hope. I will find a way." And so he strove to ease their fears.

Soon the king arrived to view the newly captured herds. He was pleased. He strung his bow in preparation for the hunt. Noticing the two deer kings below, he said, "The leaders of both herds are magnificent animals. No one is to shoot them. They shall be spared." Then, standing on the wall, looking down over the stockade, he sent his arrows flying into the milling herds. The deer became frantic. Racing wildly they injured one another with horns and hooves as they sought to escape the deadly rain of arrows.

And so it went. Every few days the king and his courtiers would return to the stockade. And every few days more of the gentle deer were killed. Many others were wounded by the flying arrows. Still others were injured in the effort to escape.

The king of the Banyan Deer met with the leader of the other herd. "Brother," he said shaking his antlered head sadly, "we are trapped. I've tried every way, but all are barred against us. The pain our subjects suffer is unbearable. As you know, when the arrows fly, many get badly hurt just trying to stay alive. Let us hold a lottery. Each day all the deer, one day from your herd, one day from mine, must pick a straw. Then, the one single deer on whom the lottery falls will go stand near the wall just below the king. That one deer must offer itself to be shot. It is a terrible solution, but at least this way we can keep many from needless injury and pain."

And the leader of the other herd agreed.

The next day, when the king and his courtiers arrived, they found one trembling deer standing directly below them. Its legs and body were shaking, but it held its head high. "What is this?" said the king. "Ah, I see. These are noble deer indeed! They have chosen that one deer alone shall die rather than that they all should suffer from our hunt. Those deer kings have wisdom." A heaviness descended on the king's heart. "We will accept their terms," he announced. "From now on shoot only the one deer that stands below." And unstringing his bow, he descended from the stockade wall and rode back in silence to the palace.

That night the king tossed and turned, a radiant deer pacing through his dreams.

One day the lot fell on a pregnant doe. She went to her king, the leader of the other herd, and said, "I will willingly go and fulfill the lottery once my fawn is safely born. But if I go now, both I and my unborn child will die. Please spare me for now. I do not ask for myself but for the sake of the child that is soon to be born."

But the leader of that herd said, "The law is the law. I cannot spare you. The lottery has fallen on you and you must die. There are no exceptions. Justice demands that you go."

In desperation she ran to the Banyan Deer. She fell on her knees before him and begged for his aid. He listened quietly, observing her with wide and gentle eyes. "Rise, Sister," said the Banyan Deer, "and go free. You are right. The terms of the lottery require that only one need die. Therefore you shall be freed from the lottery until your fawn is born. I will see that it is so done."

Too overjoyed for words, the grateful doe bowed and, then, bounded away.

The Banyan Deer King rose to his feet. There was no other he could send to take her place. He had spared her, therefore he himself must replace her. How could it be otherwise?

He walked calmly, with great dignity, through his browsing herd.

They watched him as he moved among them. His great, curving antlers and strong shoulders, his shining eyes and sharp, black hooves, all reassured and comforted them. Never had their Banyan Deer King let them down. Never had he abandoned them. If there was a way, he would find it. If there was a chance to save another, he would take it. Not once had he lorded it over them.

He was a king indeed, and his whole herd took comfort in his presence.

The courtiers were waiting with bows drawn atop the stockade. When they saw it was the Deer King who had come to stand below, they called out, "O King of the Banyan Deer, you know our king has spared you. Why are you here?"

"I have come so that two others need not die. Now shoot! You have your work and I have mine."

But, lowering their bows, they sent a message to the king. "Your Majesty, come with all speed to the stockade."

Not long after, the king arrived, riding like the wind, with his robes streaming behind him.

"What is it?" he called. "Why have you summoned me?"

"Come your majesty," his men called. "Look!"

Dismounting from his horse, the king hurried up the rough wooden steps and looked down over the wall.

The Banyan Deer stood below. Then deer king and human king looked at one another.

"Banyan King," said the King of Men at last, "I know you. I have seen you gliding through the forests of my dreams. Why are you here? Have I not freed you from my hunt?"

"Great King," replied the Banyan Deer, "what ruler can be free if the people suffer? Today a doe with fawn asked for my aid. The lottery had fallen on her and both she and her unborn fawn were to die. The lottery requires that only one shall die. I shall be that one. I shall take her place. The lottery shall be fulfilled. This is my right and my duty as king."

A stone rolled from the king's heart. "Noble Banyan Deer," he said, "you are right. A king should care for the least of his subjects. It is a lesson I have been long in the learning, but today, through your sacrifice, you have made it clear to me. So I shall give you a gift, a teacher's fee for the lesson you have taught me. You and your whole herd are freed. None of you shall be hunted again. Go and live in peace."

But the Banyan Deer said, "Great King, that is, indeed, a noble gift. But I cannot leave yet. May I speak further?"

"Speak on, Noble Deer."

"O King of Men, if I depart to safety with my own herd, will that not mean that the remaining herd shall simply suffer all the more? Each day you shall kill only them. They will have no respite. A rain of arrows will fall upon them. While I desire, above all things, the safety of my people, I cannot buy it at the cost of increasing the suffering of others. Do you understand?"

The human king was stunned. "What!?" he exclaimed. "Would you, then, risk your own and your herd's freedom for others?"

"Yes," said the Banyan Deer, "I would. I will. Think of their anguish, Great King. Imagine their sufferings, and then let them too go free."

The King of Men paused and he pondered. At last he lifted his head and smiled. "Never have I seen such nobility or such resolute concern. How can I refuse you? You shall have your wish. The other herd too shall go free. Now, can you go off with your own herd and be at peace?"

But the Banyan Deer answered, "No, Great King, I cannot. I think of all the other wild, four-footed creatures. Like them, I have lived my life surrounded by dangers and by fears. How could I live in peace knowing the terrors they must endure? I beg you, Mighty King, have pity on them. There can be no peace unless they too are free."

The King of Men was again astonished. He had never imagined such a thing. He thought and thought, and slowly the truth of the Banyan Deer's words grew clear to him. It was true, he realized. There is no real peace unless its benefits extend to all.

"You are right, Great Deer," said the King of Men at last. "Never again, in all my realm, shall any four-footed creature be slain. They are all freed from my hunt—rabbit, boar, bear, lion, leopard, tiger, deer—all. Never again shall they fall to my huntsmen's arrows. So, my Teacher, have you now found peace?"

But the Banyan Deer said, "No, Great King, I have not. What, my Lord, of the defenseless ones of the air? The birds, Great King, live surrounded by a net of danger. Stones and arrows shall greet them now wherever they fly. They shall fall from the skies like a rain throughout your kingdom. They shall know such suffering as can hardly be imagined. O Great King, I beg you. Let them go free. Release them also."

"Great One," said the King of Men, "You drive a hard bargain and are determined, it seems, to make farmers of us all. But, yes, I shall free the birds. They may now fly freely throughout my realm. No man shall hunt them again. Then may they build their nests in peace. Now, are you satisfied? Are you at last at peace?"

"Great King," answered the Banyan Deer, "think if you will of the silent ones of your realm—the fish, my Lord. If I do not now speak for them, who will? While they swim the lakes, rivers, and streams of your land, hooks, nets, and spears will be ever poised above them. How can I have peace while they abide in such danger? Great King, I beg you, spare them as well."

"Noble Being," said the King of Men, tears trickling down his cheeks. "Compassionate One, never before have I been moved to think in such a way, but, yes, I do so agree. The fish, too, are of my kingdom, and they, too, shall be free. They shall swim throughout my land, and no one shall kill them again.

"Now, all of you assembled courtiers and attendants," announced the king, "hear my words; this is my proclamation. See that it is posted throughout the land. From this day forth, all beings in my realm shall be recognized as my own dear subjects. None shall be trapped, hunted, or killed. This is my lasting decree. See to it that it is fulfilled.

"Now, tell me, Noble One," he said, turning to the Banyan Deer once more, "are you at peace?"

Flocks of birds flew overhead and perched, singing, from among the nearby trees. Deer grazed calmly on the green grass.

"Yes," said the Banyan Deer, "Now I am at peace!" And he leaped up, kicking like a fawn. He leaped for joy—sheer joy! He had saved them all!

Then he thanked the king and, gathering his herd, departed with his herd back into the depths of the forest.

The king had a stone pillar set on the spot where he had spoken with the Banyan Deer. Carved upon it was the figure of a deer, encircled with these words: "Homage to the Noble Banyan Deer, Compassionate Teacher of Kings."

Then he too lived on, caring wisely for all things.

Early Buddhist

A Tale for all Seasons

"Tell me the weight of a snowflake," a coal-mouse asked a wild dove.
"Nothing more than nothing," was the answer.
"In that case, I must tell you a marvelous story," the coal-mouse said.

"I sat on the branch of a fir, close to its trunk, when it began to snow—not heavily, not in a raging blizzard—no, just like a dream, without a sound and without any violence. Since I did not have anything better to do, I counted the snowflakes settling on the twigs and needles of my branch. Their number was exactly 3,741,952. When the 3,741,953rd dropped onto the branch, nothing more than nothing, as you say—the branch broke off."

Having said that, the coal-mouse flew away.

The dove, since Noah's time an authority on the matter, thought about the story for awhile, and finally said to herself, "Perhaps there is only one person's voice lacking for peace to come to the world."

Kurt Kauter, *New Fables, Thus Spoke "The Carabou"*

One day as I was walking along Marylebone Road I was suddenly seized with an extraordinary sense of great joy and exaltation as though a marvellous beam of spiritual power had shot through me linking me in rapture with the world, the universe, life with a capital L, and all the beings around me. All delight and power, all things living, all time fused in a brief second.

Meg Maxwell and Verena Tschudin, *Seeing the Invisible*
from The Alister Hardy Research Center

I slept
and I dreamt that life was all joy.
I awoke
and saw that life was but service.
I served
and understood that service was joy.

R. Tagore

Chapter II

The Pilgrimage

Two children lived with their mother on the outskirts of a high mountain village. The children had never met their father. They had an intense desire to be united with him. They pleaded with their mother to take them to see him, but she kept putting them off. She told them that it would not be easy to reach their father. They would have to cross over several mountain ranges and through deep forests. There would be many precarious rivers in their path which would be difficult to cross.

But the children were so intent on being with their father, that day after day they asked when they could begin their journey. Seeing the intensity of the children's desire, the mother could resist no longer. "We will start when we have properly *prepared* ourselves," she said, "when we have the proper provisions, food and warm clothing, when we are physically and mentally ready for the hardships we will face, then we will go." They all worked diligently to prepare. They lived more austerely, giving up many small pleasures in order to obtain the necessary provisions, but they found an even greater joy in what they were accomplishing together. Finally, when the day came for them to depart, the children were overjoyed.

For the next several months, they endured many hardships. They were often exhausted or hungry, but they persevered. They traveled hundreds of miles on foot over difficult terrain. At last they came to a plateau that looked vaguely familiar. Pointing to a house in the distance, the mother said, "That is where your father lives, now you will meet him." The children could hardly believe that they had almost arrived at their longed for goal. As they approached the house and knocked on the door, they could hardly stand the anticipation.

When their father came out, he was as overjoyed as the children. He took them in his arms and brought them inside, where they played together through the day, singing, dancing, telling stories, and being at home. He had many presents to give them. Later as the sun was setting, the children became sleepy. Their father pointed to a door, telling them that in the next room they would find warm, comfortable beds. Tired but content, the children opened the door. When they went into the next room they were surprised to find that they were in their own house, and that their father had been living unseen, right next to them all the time.

The Song of the Bird

The disciples were full of questions about God.

Said the master, "God is the Unknown and the Unknowable. Every statement about him, every answer to your questions, is a distortion of the truth."

The disciples were bewildered. "Then why do you speak about him at all?"

"Why does the bird sing?" said the master.

Christian

Ask, and it shall be given to you; seek, and you shall find; knock, and it shall be opened to you.

For whoever asks, receives; and he who seeks, finds; and to him who knocks, the door is opened.

The Gospel According to Saint Matthew

The Beloved

One went to the door of the Beloved and knocked.
A voice asked, "Who is there?"
He answered, "It is I."
The voice said, "There is no room for Me and Thee."
The door was shut.
After a year of solitude and deprivation, he returned and knocked.
A voice from within asked, "Who is there?"

The man said, "It is Thee."
The door was opened for him.

Jalaluddin Rumi

ᘓᗉᘓᗉᘓᗉᘓᗉᘓᗉᘓ

The Road Not Taken

Two roads diverged in a wood, and I—
I took the one less traveled by,
And that has made all the difference.

Robert Frost

ᘓᗉᘓᗉᘓᗉᘓᗉᘓᗉᘓ

Rag-Tag Army

I think God must be very old and very tired. Maybe he used to look splendid and fine in his general's uniform, but no more. He's been on the march a long time, you know. And look at his rag-tag little army! All he has for soldiers are you and me. Dumb little army. Listen! The drum beat isn't even regular. Everyone is out of step. And there! You see? God keeps stopping along the way to pick up one of his tinier soldiers who decided to wander off and play with a frog, or run in a field, or whose foot got tangled in the underbrush. He'll never get anywhere that way. And yet, the march goes on.

Do you see how the marchers have broken up into little groups? Look at that group up near the front. Now, there's a snappy outfit. They all look pretty much alike—at least they're in step with each other. That's something! Only they're not wearing their shoes. They're carrying them in their hands. Silly little band. They won't get far before God will have to stop again.

Or how about that other group over there? They're all holding hands as they march. The only trouble with this is the men on each end of the line. Pretty soon they realize that one of their hands isn't holding onto anything—one hand is reaching, empty, alone. And so they hold hands with each other, and everybody marches around in circles. The more people holding hands, the bigger the circle. And, of course, a bigger circle is deceptive because as we march along it looks like we're going someplace, but we're not. And so God must stop again. You see what I mean? He'll never get anywhere that way!

If God were more sensible he'd take his little army and shape them up. Why, whoever heard of a soldier stopping to romp in a field? It's ridiculous. But even more absurd is a general who will stop the march of eternity to go and bring him back. But that's God for you. His is no endless, empty marching. He is going somewhere. His steps are deliberate and purposive. He may be old, and he may be tired. But he knows where he's going. And he means to take every last one of his tiny soldiers with him. Only there aren't going to be any forced marches. And, after all, there are frogs and flowers, and thorns and underbrush along the way. And even though our foreheads have been signed with the sign of the cross, we are only human. And most of us are afraid and lonely and would like to hold hands or cry or run away. And we don't know where we are going, and we can't seem to trust God—especially when it's dark out and we can't see him! And he won't go on without us. And that's why it's taking so long.

Listen! The drum beat isn't even regular. Everyone is out of step. And there! You see? God keeps stopping along the way to pick up one of his tinier soldiers who decided to wander off and play with a frog, or run in a field, or whose foot got tangled in the underbrush. He'll never get anywhere that way!

And yet, the march goes on . . .

Martin Bell

ê🐦ê🐦ê🐦ê🐦ê🐦ê🐦

Do you need proof of God? Does one light a torch to see the sun?

Oriental Wisdom

ê🐦ê🐦ê🐦ê🐦ê🐦ê🐦

Seek ye first the kingdom of heaven, and all else shall be added unto you.

The Gospel According to Saint Matthew

ê🐦ê🐦ê🐦ê🐦ê🐦ê🐦

You are an adolescent shepherd in a tiny English village, in Sussex. Each day you take your flock to the hills, where you lie on your back, searching out images in the cloud formations, one ear always cocked for sounds of possible danger.

One afternoon, you return to find your village astir with anticipation. A stranger has arrived, a pilgrim returning from the great shrine at Canterbury. In exchange for a meal and a night's lodging, the stranger will sit at the village fire that evening and tell the tale of his travels. Eagerly, you join in the preparations. At the supper, you are so anxious to hear the pilgrim's story that you gulp rather than savor the rare rich meal. Ages seem to pass before everyone is finished eating, and the site is tidied. As the villagers settle in to hear the traveler's tale, you scramble to gain a place near the front so that you can see and follow the expressions on his face.

The stranger begins, recounting both the perils and the happy coincidences of his journey, describing his fellow-pilgrims, and finally detailing the magnificence of the great shrine of Canterbury and the wonders to be beheld there. You hang on every word, picturing every nuance of his story in your imagination. Long after the story is over and you lie abed in your hut, your mind leaps into those pictures, trying to make the stranger's adventures a part of your own life. The next day, as you return to the hillside with your flock, you see in the clouds the shapes described by the storyteller, and you long to make a similar pilgrimage. But that is impossible. Young shepherds whose work is needed to help sustain their families do not make pilgrimages.

Several months later, a sheep-plague strikes the area, and most of the villagers' sheep die. You soon realize that you have become more a liability than an asset to your family and that for their sake as well as your own, you must make your way to the great city of London, perhaps to learn some new skill, at least to find a way of living.

But you need not go to the city directly or at once. Indeed, for your spiritual welfare as well as to ask God's blessings on your ambitions, you decide to journey by way of Canterbury, finally making the long-dreamed of pilgrimage. But how to get there? There are no maps; only barons and their knights have those. Still, you do not worry, for starting out is simple: There is but one road through your village, and you know the direction from which the stranger came.

You also know the habits of pilgrims—how your stranger had stopped in a similar way the evening before arriving in your village. After a day's journey, you might be fortunate enough to stop where he had stopped, and there you might find someone who can point you in the right direction for the next leg of your own pilgrimage. And so you set off, not knowing exactly where you are going nor exactly how to get there, but hoping to find on the way others who are interested in the same quest and who can help to guide your own.

And, of course, you do. Travelers are rare in that age, and strangers rarely meet except when traveling. The people you meet thus answer the question, "Who are you?" by detailing "how I come to be *here*." Each person who joins the quest tells *how* she heard of the goal and *what* he knows of it. In the process of telling the stories of their lives, the pilgrims band together, pooling their knowledge about the journey, merging bits of wisdom remembered from the stories told by others who had made the same journey. "The route through that wood is attacked by robbers." "The rockier trail is the best way around the hill." "After a rain, that stream can be forded only above its rapids." In less stressful moments, the journeyers share expectations and hopes: "I heard that a man with a leg more crippled than mine was cured." "When the procession of the Sacrament begins, it is as if the angels were singing." "Even lawyers have become humble when standing at that altar."

Thus it is that, on the way, you learn more not only about the goal you are seeking—the Canterbury of Becket, who preferred the risk of a king's wrath to the risk of God's judgment—but also about yourself as the seeker of that goal. What risks are you willing to take? Which do you refuse? What kind of people have hopes such as your own? Whom would you like to be like? Whose help do you accept? Whose do you suspect?

And, of course, the paramount discovery gradually dawns as the pilgrimage continues—the realization that the ultimate goal you seek is not some reality "out there," but the awakening of an identity that lies *within*.

Christian

The Only Path

"Everything is laid out for you. Your path is straight ahead of you. Sometimes it's invisible but it's there. You may not know where it's going, but still you have to follow that path. It's the path to the Creator. That's the only path there is."

Leon Shenandoah, Native American Elder
Six Nations Iroquois Confederacy

Where are you searching for me, friend?
Look! Here am I right within you.
Not in temple, nor in mosque,
Not in Kaaba, nor Kailas,
But here right within you am I.

Kabir

You are in the world of things that come to be, and yet you seek to be at rest. But how can anything be at rest in the world of things that come to be? A boat, as long as it floats on the water, cannot be still or at rest; or if at any moment it is still, it is so only by chance, and forthwith the water begins again to shake and toss the things which float upon its surface. Then only is the boat at rest, when it is taken out of the water, and drawn up on the land, which is the place of the boat's origin, and is on a par with the boat in density and weight; then, but not till then, is the boat truly at rest. And even so, the soul, as long as it is involved in the processes of the physical world, cannot be still, nor be at rest, nor get any respite; but if it returns to its source and root, then it is still and is at rest, and reposes from the misery and debasement of its wandering in a foreign land.

Hermes Trismegistus

ළඔළඔළඔළඔළඔළඔ

Drop Your Nothing

Disciple: I have come to you with nothing in my hands.
Master: Then drop it at once!
Disciple: But how can I drop it? It is nothing.
Master: Then carry it around with you!

ළඔළඔළඔළඔළඔළඔ

[T]hose who want to journey on this road . . . must have a great and very resolute determination to persevere until reaching the end, come what may, happen what may, whatever work is involved, whatever criticism arises, whether they die on the road, or even if the whole world collapses. You will hear some people frequently making objections: "there are dangers"; "this one was deceived"; "another who prayed a great deal fell away"; "it is harmful to virtue"; "it is not for women for they will be susceptible to illusions"; "it is better they stick to their sewing"; "they don't need these delicacies"; "the Our Father and the Hail Mary are sufficient." . . . [D]on't pay any attention to the fears they raise or to the picture of the dangers they paint for you . . . . Sisters, give up these fears; never pay attention in like matters to the opinion of the crowd. Behold these are not the times to believe everyone; believe only those who you see are walking in conformity with Christ's life.

Saint Teresa of Ávila

ළඔළඔළඔළඔළඔළඔ

If a man is crossing a river
And an empty boat collides with his own skiff,
Even though he be a bad-tempered man
He will not become very angry.
But if he sees a man in the boat,
He will shout at him to steer clear.
If the shout is not heard, he will shout again,
And yet again, and begin cursing.
And all because there is somebody in the boat.
Yet if the boat were empty,
He would not be shouting, and not angry.

If you can empty your own boat
Crossing the river of the world,

No one will oppose you,
No one will seek to harm you.

Chuang Tzu

お・お・お・お・お・お

As I looked about the world, so much of it impoverished, I became increasingly uncomfortable about having so much while my brothers and sisters were starving. Finally, I had to find another way. The turning point came when, in desperation and out of a very deep seeking for a meaningful way of life, I walked all one night through the woods. I came to a moonlit glade and prayed.

I felt a complete willingness, without any reservations, to give my life—to dedicate my life—to service. "Please use me!" I prayed to God. And a great peace came over me.

I tell you it's a point of no return. After that, you can never go back to completely self-centered living.

And so I went into the second phase of my life. I began to live to *give* what I could, instead of to get what I could, and I entered a new and wonderful world. My life began to be meaningful. I attained the great blessing of good health; I haven't had an ache or pain, a cold or headache since. (Most illness, you know, is psychologically induced.) From that time on, I have known that my life work would be for peace—that it would cover the *whole peace picture:* peace among nations, peace among groups, peace among individuals, and the very, very important inner peace.

Peace Pilgrim

お・お・お・お・お・お

In the remote mountains of northern Greece, there once lived a monk who had desired all of his life to make a pilgrimage to the Holy Sepulchre—to walk three times around it, to kneel, and to return home a new person. Gradually, through the years, he had saved what money he could, begging in the villages nearby, and finally, near the end of his life, had enough set aside to begin his trip. He opened the gates of the monastery and, staff in hand, set out with great anticipation on his way to Jerusalem.

But no sooner had he left the cloister than he encountered a man in rags, sad and bent to the ground, picking herbs. "Where are you going, Father?" the man asked. "To the Holy Sepulchre, brother. By God's grace, I shall walk three times around it, kneel, and return home a different man from what I am."

"How much money to do that do you have, Father?" inquired the man. "Thirty pounds," the monk answered. "Give me the thirty pounds," said the beggar. "I have a wife and hungry children. Give me the money, walk three times around me, then kneel and go back into your monastery."

The monk thought for a moment, scratching the ground with his staff, then took the thirty pounds from his sack, gave the whole of it to the poor man, walked three times around him, knelt, and went back through the gates of his monastery.

He returned home a new person, of course, having recognized that the beggar was Christ himself—not in some magical place far away, but right outside his monastery door, mysteriously close. In abandoning his quest for the remote, the special, the somehow "magical," the monk discovered a meaning far more profound in the ordinary experience close to home. All that he had given up came suddenly rushing back to him with a joy unforeseen.

To be surprised by grace is a gift still to be prized.

Retold by Nikos Kazantzakis

🐤🐤🐤🐤🐤🐤

When life itself seems lunatic, who knows where madness lies? To surrender dreams . . . this may be madness. Too much sanity may be madness and, the maddest of all, to see life as it is and not as it should be.

Don Quixote

🐤🐤🐤🐤🐤🐤

The Duckling

I have been considered a misfit since my childhood. No one seemed to understand me. My own father once said to me, "You are not mad enough to be put in a madhouse, and not withdrawn enough to be put in a monastery. I don't know what to do with you."

I replied, "A duck's egg was once put under a hen. When the egg hatched the duckling walked about with the mother hen until they came to a pond. The duckling went straight into the water. The hen stayed clucking anxiously on land. Now, dear father, I have walked into the ocean and find in it my home. You can hardly blame me if you choose to stay on the shore."

Sufi, *Shams of Tabriz*

🐤🐤🐤🐤🐤🐤

The Way of Wisdom:

He who knows not, and knows not that he knows not, is a fool.

Shun him.

He who knows not, and knows that he knows not, is a child.

Teach him.

He who knows, and knows not that he knows, is asleep.

Wake him.

He who knows, and knows that he knows, is wise.

Follow him.

Unknown Persian philosopher

እ‑እ‑እ‑እ‑እ‑እ‑

The disciple, the would-be initiate, approaches the master and says: "Teach me."

And the teacher replies: "Come, *follow* me."

Sometimes, the newcomer tries to insist: "No, I mean *tell* me."

And the adept can only smile a welcoming love that cannot be "told."

More often, like the good and intelligent aspirant in Luke's gospel, the now-no-longer-neophyte turns sadly away.

Spirituality is a reality that one approaches not by "learning," but by *following*.

እ‑እ‑እ‑እ‑እ‑እ‑

The Master

It is related by a Sufi master that, when he was a youth, he wanted to attach himself to a teaching master. He sought the sage, and asked to become his disciple.

The teacher said: 'You are not yet ready.'

Since the young man was insistent, the sage said: 'Very well, I will teach you something. I am going on a pilgrimage to Mecca. Come with me.'

The disciple was overjoyed.

'Since we are traveling companions,' said the teacher, 'one must lead, and the other obey. Choose your role.'

'I will follow, you lead,' said the disciple.

'If you know how to follow,' said the master.

The journey started. While they were resting one night in the desert of the Hejaz, it started to rain. The master got up and held a covering over the disciple, protecting him.

'But this is what *I* should be doing for you,' said the disciple.

'I command you to allow me to protect you thus,' said the sage.

When it was day the young man said: 'Now it is a new day. Let *me* be the leader, and you follow me.' The master agreed.

'I shall now collect brushwood, to make a fire,' said the youth.

'You may do no such thing; I shall collect it,' said the sage.

'I command you to sit there while I collect brushwood!' said the young man.

'You may do no such thing,' said the teacher, 'for it is not in accordance with the requirements of discipleship for the follower to allow himself to be served by the leader.'

And so, on every occasion, the Master showed the student what discipleship really meant, by demonstration.

They parted at the gate of the Holy City. Seeing the sage later, the young man could not meet his eyes. 'That which you have learned,' said the older man, 'is something of the nature of discipleship.'

The disciple must know *how* to obey, not merely that he must obey. The question of *whether* to become a disciple or not only comes after the person knows what discipleship really is. People spend their time wondering whether they should be disciples—or otherwise. Since their assumption (that they could be a disciple if they wished it) is incorrect, they are living in a false world, an intellectualist world. Such people have not learned the first lesson.

Sufi

True Spirituality

The master was asked, "What is spirituality?"

He said, "Spirituality is that which succeeds in bringing one to inner transformation."

"But if I apply the traditional methods handed down by the masters, is that not spirituality?"

"It is not spirituality if it does not perform its function for you. A blanket is no longer a blanket if it does not keep you warm."

"So spirituality does change?"

"People change and needs change. So what was spirituality once is spirituality no more. What generally goes under the name of spirituality is merely the record of past methods."

Sufi

Once a murshid had been to the city, and on his return he said, "Oh, I am filled with joy, I am filled with joy. There was such an exaltation in the presence of the Beloved." Then his mureed thought, "There was a beloved and an exaltation; how wonderful! I must go and see if I cannot find one also."

He went through the city, and he came back and said, "Horrible! How terrible the world is! All seem to be at one another's throats; that was the picture I saw. I felt nothing but depression, as if my whole being was torn to pieces." "Yes," the murshid said, "you are right." But explain to me," the mureed said, "why you are so exalted after going out, and why I am so torn to pieces. I cannot bear it; it is horrible." The murshid said, "You did not walk in the rhythm that I walked in through the city."

Sufi

Guatama Buddha, the Illumined One, was in meditation in the Himalayas. Many months and years had already passed, and he yet remained in his state of meditation. Came winds, came rains, the winds blew earth upon his body, little seeds fell there and the grass began to grow. There came two swallows who built a nest upon his shoulder. The swallows came back every year to their nest for many years, but one spring they did not return. Then in the eyes of the Buddha, the perfect one, who was at the door of Nirvana to which he had been invited by the gods, appeared tears, for he missed the swallows. And the Buddha discovered that he was not yet ready to enter the door of Nirvana; there was yet suffering in his heart, and he returned among men to teach them the path.

Buddhist

The Water-melon Hunter

Once upon a time there was a man who strayed, from his own country, into the world known as the Land of Fools.

He soon saw a number of people flying in terror from a field where they had been trying to reap wheat. 'There is a monster in that field,' they told him. He looked, and saw that it was a water-melon.

He offered to kill the 'monster' for them. When he had cut the melon from its stalk, he took a slice and began to eat it. The people became even more terrified of him than they had been of the melon. They drove him away with pitchforks, crying: 'He will kill us next, unless we get rid of him.'

It so happened that at another time another man also strayed into the Land of Fools, and the same thing started to happen to him. But, instead of offering to help them with the 'monster,' he agreed with them that it must be dangerous, and, by tiptoeing away from it with them, he gained their confidence. He spent a long time with them in their houses until he could teach them, little by little, the basic facts which would enable them not only to lose their fear of melons, but even to cultivate them themselves.

Mention is made of two classes of yogis: hidden and the known. Those who have renounced the world are the "known" yogis: all recognize them. But the "hidden" yogis live in the world. They are not known.

Sri Ramakrishna, *The Gospel of Sri Ramakrishna*

 za za za za za

There was an occasion when I felt that I was indeed battling with the elements. It was my experience of walking through a dust storm which sometimes blew with such force I could scarcely stand against it, while sometimes the dust was so thick I could not see ahead and could only guide myself by the edge of the road. A policeman stopped alongside me, threw open his car door and yelled, "Get in here, woman, before you get killed." I told him I was walking a pilgrimage and did not accept rides (at that time). I also told him that God was my shield and there was nothing to fear. At that moment the winds died down, the dust settled and the sun broke from the clouds. I continued to walk. But the wonderful thing was that I felt spiritually lifted above the hardship.

Peace Pilgrim

za za za za za

Once, when Vîshtâspa, King of Persia, was returning from a victorious campaign, he came near to the place where Zoroaster lived and taught his disciples. He decided to visit the famous man, whose name was known to every Persian, and to see if he could answer those difficult questions which the wise men in his palace were unable to explain.

The king and his retinue turned aside to Zoroaster's place and saw a man who seemed to be a teacher, with a group of disciples round him. All were busy in an orchard and the Master appeared to be instructing them. At the king's approach, the disciples withdrew.

Then the king said to Zoroaster: "I believe you to be the great Zoroaster and I have come that you may explain to me the laws of nature and the universe. If you are as wise a man as my people declare, this will doubtless not take you long. I cannot tarry, as I am on my way home from a war and important matters of state await me at my palace."

Looking at the king, Zoroaster took a grain of wheat from the earth and gave it to him. "In this small grain of wheat," he declared, "are contained all the laws of the universe and the forces of nature." The king was much astonished by this answer, which he did not understand. And when he saw smiles on the faces of those around him, he was angry and threw the grain upon the ground, thinking that he was being mocked. And to Zoroaster he said: "I believed that you were a wise man and a great philosopher, but I now see that you are a stubborn and ignorant man, hiding your ignorance beneath the cloak of exaggeration. I was foolish to waste my time by coming here to see you." And with that the king turned to depart and rode on to his palace.

Then Zoroaster picked up the grain of wheat, saying to his disciples: "I will keep this grain of wheat, because it will one day be needed by the king and will be his teacher."

The years passed. The king was successful as ruler and warrior, and led a life of luxury and apparent contentment in his palace. But at night, when he went to bed, strange thoughts came into his mind and troubled him.

"I live in luxury and abundance in this splendid palace," thought the king, "but not far away are multitudes of people who live in misery and want, who are cold and are hungry. Why am I king? Why do I have power over all men and all things in my empire? Why are the people poor and why do they suffer? How long shall I enjoy this abundance and power, and what will happen to me when I die? Can my power and my riches save me from illness and death? What will they avail when I lie in my grave? What will happen when my body turns to dust and feeds the worms? Will aught be left of this life or is everything lost with the coming of death? If I pass on to another life, shall I still be myself, or shall I be someone entirely different? And if there is another life, what shall I experience in it? Shall I continue to have the power and riches of my present life, or shall I be a vagabond with no place to lay my head, exposed to all the inclemency of nature and lacking money for the morrow's food? What happened before I came into this life? Did I live before in this country or in another? Or was I born for the first time into this life? How did life begin? How did the world come into being, and what was there before life appeared? What was there before the creation of the universe? Was the universe created by someone, and was that someone God? Who created God? What is time? What existed before time? Does eternity exist? If so, how can we conceive eternity?"

The nights of the king were tormented by such questions, and often he did not sleep till morning came.

No one in the palace could answer these questions, but meanwhile the fame of Zoroaster grew. The king was aware that many disciples were coming to the teacher from many lands, and he felt that there was the man who might be able to tell him more of these problems than anyone else. So putting by his pride, he dispatched a great caravan of treasure to Zoroaster and with it an invitation and a request. "I regret," he wrote, "that when I was impatient and thoughtless in my youth, I asked you to explain the great problems of existence in a few minutes of time. I have changed and do not want the impossible. But I am still deeply interested to know the laws of the universe and the forces of nature, even more so than when I was a young man. Come to my palace, I pray you, or if that is not possible, then send to me the best of your disciples that he may teach me all that he can about these questions."

After an interval the caravan and the messengers returned. These told the king that they had found Zoroaster, who sent him greeting but returned the proffered treasure. The treasure, Zoroaster had said, was of no use to a gardener, but he was glad to keep the wrappings of the packages, as they would be useful to protect his trees and plants against the cold of winter. Moreover, Zoroaster had sent the king a gift wrapped in a leaf and had asked the messengers to tell him that this was the teacher who would teach him everything concerning the forces of nature and the laws of the universe. "I am not sending one of my disciples," Zoroaster had said, "but my own teacher who has taught me all I know about the laws of life. I trust that the king will be as apt to learn as my teacher is to teach."

Then the king asked where the teacher was and in reply the messengers handed him the little gift wrapped in the leaf. The king opened it and found the same grain of wheat that Zoroaster had given him before. He was greatly perturbed by the wheat and thought there must be something mysterious and magical in it. So he put it in a golden box and hid it among his treasures. Almost every day he looked at it, expecting some miracle to happen, such as the turning of the grain of wheat into something or someone that would teach him all he wished to know.

Months went by, but nothing happened. At last the king lost patience and said: "It seems that Zoroaster has deceived me again. Either he is making a mock of me or else he does not know the answers to my questions. I will show him that I can find the answers without his help." So the king sent a caravan to the great Indian philosopher Tshengregacha, to whom came disciples from all parts of the world, and with the caravan went the same messengers and the same treasure that he had once sent to Zoroaster.

After many months the messengers returned from India and announced that the philosopher had consented to become the king's teacher and would soon arrive at his court. Then the king was glad and ordered that festivities be held in honour of his guest and, when the philosopher arrived, he thanked him for coming from such a far country.

But Tshengregacha said to him: "I am honoured to be your teacher, but in frankness must tell you that I come chiefly to your country that I may meet the great Zoroaster, of whom I have heard such wide report. Indeed I do not know why you should have need of me when you are so near to one who can doubtless tell you more than I." Then the king took the golden box containing the grain of wheat and answered: "I asked Zoroaster to teach me; see, this is what he sent me. Here is the teacher who shall teach me the laws of the universe and the forces of nature. Is this not ridiculous? How can as great a teacher as you think Zoroaster to be commit such folly?"

Tshengregacha looked long at the grain of wheat and silence fell upon the palace while he meditated. At length he said: "I do not regret my many months of journeying, for now I know that Zoroaster is in truth the great teacher that I have long believed him to be. This tiny grain of wheat can indeed teach us the laws of the universe and the forces of nature, for it contains them in itself. Even as you must not keep the grain of wheat in its golden box if you would learn the answers to the weighty questions which trouble you and if you would grow in wisdom and understanding, so you yourself must not stay in this luxurious palace. If you plant this little grain in the earth where it belongs, in contact with the soil, the rain, the air, the sunshine and the light of the moon and of the stars, then, like a universe in itself, it will begin to grow bigger and bigger. Likewise you, if you would grow in knowledge and understanding, must leave this artificial palace and go into your garden, where you will be close to all the forces of nature and of the universe—to the sum total of things. Just as inexhaustible sources of energy are ever flowing towards the grain planted in the earth, so will innumerable sources of knowledge open and flow towards you, till you become one with nature and the organic universe. If you watch the growth of this seed of grain you will find that there is an indestructible and mysterious power in it—the power of life. If you watch long enough, you will see that the grain disappears and is replaced by a plant which will triumph over all obstacles and opposition—which will grow higher and higher because it has life within it. If you throw a stone upwards, it falls again to the ground, since it is dead and not living and has not the mysterious power of life which enables the plant to grow higher and higher and to triumph over death. At the moment when the grain sprouts, there is victory over death, and indeed at every instant of the plant's growth towards the sun in the face of great opposing forces."

"All that you say is true," answered the king, "yet in the end the plant will wither and die and will be dissolved in the earth."

"But not," said the philosopher, "until it has done an act of creation and has turned itself into hundreds of grains each like the first. The tiny grain disappeared as it grew into a plant, and you, too, as you grow, must turn yourself into something and someone else. In the same way a great truth also seems to disappear and be turned into something that is seemingly different, but only to return in a greater form, like the hundred grains that take the place of the one.

"You, too, must one day cease to be your present self, so that you may become a richer personality, in pursuance of the law that life always creates more life, truth more abundant truth, the seed more abundant seeds. This is one answer to your problems given by the grain of wheat. It teaches that everything is in movement and is constantly changing and growing; that life and all things else are the result of struggle between two opposite forces. If you go into your garden and will look at soil and rain, at the sky and the sun and the stars, they will teach you many more truths of a like kind.

"The grain of wheat is indeed a great teacher. We should be thankful to Zoroaster for having sent it to us. I propose that now we go to rest and that on the morrow we journey to Zoroaster himself that he may teach us more of these things. He will be able to tell you all that you wish to know of the matters which trouble you, and I myself will profit from his wisdom."

The king was much moved by Tshengregacha's words and readily agreed to his suggestion. In a few days' time they came to the garden of Zoroaster and understood at once the method by which he taught his disciples. His only book was the great book of nature, and he taught his disciples to read in it.

The two visitors learned another great truth in Zoroaster's garden: that life and work, study and leisure, are one and the same; that the right way to live is a simple, natural life—a creative life within which individual growth is a single total dynamism. They spent a year in the garden, learning to read the laws of existence and of Life from the vast book of nature. At the end of that time, the king returned to his own city and asked Zoroaster to set out systematically the essence of his great teaching. Zoroaster did so, and the result was the sacred book of the *Zend Avestas*, which by the king's command became the official religion of the Persian empire. Meanwhile Tshengregacha went back to India and there, being a poet as well as philosopher, he summed up all that he had learnt in Zoroaster's garden in the beautiful hymns of the *Rig-Veda*, another of the great sacred books of the East.

Edmond Bordeaux Szekely

For those who wish to climb the mountain of spiritual awareness, the path is selfless work. For those who have attained the summit of union with the Lord, the path is stillness and peace.

Sri Krishna, *Bhagavad Gita*

. . . Do like the bees, who never quit a flower so long as they can extract any honey from it. If, after a little hesitation and trial, you do not succeed with one consideration according to your wishes, proceed to another. But go calmly and tranquilly in this matter without hurrying yourself.

Saint Francis de Sales, *Introduction to the Devout Life*

In the sea of life,
In the sea of death
My soul, tired
In both, seeks
     The Mountain
From which the waters have receded.

Japan, Seventh Century

Chapter III

Who Am I?

Once some disciples of the Baal Shem Tov approached him and asked: "Why do you answer all questions by telling a story? Why do you always tell stories?"

The disciples then steeled themselves, certain that, true to the tradition, the Baal Shem Tov would necessarily answer such questions about story with a story.

But the Baal Shem Tov, after a loving, lingering pause responded: "Salvation lies in remembrance."

Hassidic Judaism

हहहहहहह

One day, according to an Eastern story, the gods decided to create the universe. They created the stars, the sun, the moon. They created the seas, the mountains, the flowers, and the clouds. Then they created human beings. At the end, they created Truth.

At this point, however, a problem arose: where should they hide Truth so that human beings would not find it right away? They wanted to prolong the adventure of the search.

"Let's put Truth on top of the highest mountain," said one of the gods. "Certainly it will be hard to find it there."

"Let's put it on the farthest star," said another.

"Let's hide it in the darkest and deepest of abysses."

45

"Let's conceal it on the secret side of the moon."

At the end, the wisest and most ancient god said, "No, we will hide Truth inside the very heart of human beings. In this way they will look for it all over the Universe, without being aware of having it inside themselves all the time."

Retold by Piero Ferrucci

❦❦❦❦❦❦❦

The seed of God is in us. Given an intelligent and hard-working farmer, it will thrive and grow up to God, whose seed it is; and accordingly its fruits will be God-nature. Pear seeds grow into pear trees, nut seeds into nut trees, and God seed into God.

Meister Eckhart

❦❦❦❦❦❦❦

A woman in a coma was dying. She suddenly had a feeling that she was taken up to heaven and stood before the Judgment Seat.

"Who are you?" a Voice said to her.

"I'm the wife of the mayor," she replied.

"I did not ask whose wife you are but who you are."

"I'm the mother of four children."

"I did not ask whose mother you are, but who you are."

"I'm a schoolteacher."

"I did not ask what your profession is but who you are."

And so it went. No matter what she replied, she did not seem to give a satisfactory answer to the question, "Who are you?"

"I'm a Christian."

"I did not ask what your religion is but who you are."

"I'm the one who went to church every day and always helped the poor and needy."

"I did not ask what you did but who you are."

She evidently failed the examination, for she was sent back to earth. When she recovered from her illness, she was determined to find out who she was. And that made all the difference.

❦❦❦❦❦❦❦

At the center of our being is a point of nothingness which is untouched by sin and by illusion, a point of pure truth, a point or spark which belongs entirely to God, which is never at our disposal, from which God disposes of our lives, which is inaccessible to the fantasies of our own mind or the brutalities of our own will.

Thomas Merton

The kingdom is within you,
    and it is without you,
If you will come to know yourselves,
    then you will be known by yourselves,
    and you will understand that
    you are sons of the Living Father.

The Gospel According to Saint Thomas

Wouldn't it show great ignorance, my daughters, if someone when asked who he was didn't know, and didn't know his father or mother or from what country he came? Well now, if this would be so extremely stupid, we are incomparably more so when we do not strive to know who we are, but limited ourselves to considering only roughly these bodies. Because we have heard and because faith tells us so, we know we have souls. But we seldom consider the precious things that can be found in this soul, or who dwells within it, or its high value.

Saint Teresa of Ávila

When we thus clear the ground and make our soul ready, without doubt God must fill up the void . . . . If you go out of yourself, without doubt he shall go in, and there will be much or little of his entering in according to how much or little you go out.

Johannes Tauler

A certain person wished to see the blessed Messenger [Mohammed] in a dream, but he seemed to be incapable of achieving this vision. He therefore approached a noble saint, imploring his advice. That noble being was an intimate friend of Allah. He said: "My son, on Friday evening you must eat a lot of salted fish, then perform your prayer and go to bed without drinking any water. Then you will see."

The man followed this advice. He spent the whole night dreaming that he was drinking from streams, fountains and springs. When morning came, he ran crying to the saint: "O Master, I did not see the Messenger. I was so thirsty that all I dreamed about was drinking from fountains and springs. I am still on fire with thirst."

The saint then told him: "So, eating salted fish gave you such a thirst that you dreamed all night of nothing but water. Now you must feel such a thirst for Allah's messenger and you will then behold his blessed beauty!"

Sufi

The first peace, which is the most important, is that which comes within the souls of men when they realize their relationship, their oneness, with the universe and all its Powers, and when they realize that at the center of the universe dwells *Wakan-Tanka* [the Supreme Being], and that this center is really everywhere, it is within each of us. This is the real Peace, and the others are but reflections of this. The second peace is that which is made between two individuals, and the third is that which is made between two nations. But above all you should understand that there can never be peace between nations until there is first known that true peace which, as I have often said, is within the souls of men.

Black Elk

Who Am I?

Who am I? They often tell me
I stepped from my cell's confinement
Calmly, cheerfully, firmly,
Like a squire from his country-house.
Who am I? They often tell me
I used to speak to my warders
Freely and friendly and clearly,
As though it were mine to command.
Who am I? They also tell me
I bore the days of misfortune
Equably, smilingly, proudly,
Like one accustomed to win.

Am I then really all that which other men tell of?
Or am I only what I myself know of myself?
Restless and longing and sick, like a bird in a cage,

Struggling for breath, as though hands were compressing my
    throat,
Yearning for colours, for flowers, for the voices of birds,
Thirsting for words of kindness, for neighbourliness,
Tossing in expectation of great events,
Powerlessly trembling for friends at infinite distance,
Weary and empty at praying, at thinking, at making,
Faint, and ready to say farewell to it all?

Who am I? This or the other?
Am I one person to-day and to-morrow another?
Am I both at once? A hypocrite before others,
And before myself a contemptibly woebegone weakling?
Or is something within me still like a beaten army,
Fleeing in disorder from victory already achieved?

Who am I? They mock me, these lonely questions of mine.
Whoever I am, Thou knowest, O God, I am Thine!

Dietrick Bonhoeffer, Letters and Papers from Prison

A Creature of Contraction and Expansion

I am a monk myself, and the one question I really wanted to ask was, "What is a monk?" Well, I finally did, but for an answer I got a most peculiar question: "Do you mean in the daytime or at night?" Now what could that mean?

When I didn't answer, he picked it up again, "A monk, like everyone else, is a creature of contraction and expansion. During the day he is contracted—behind his cloister walls, dressed in a habit like all the others, doing the routine things you expect a monk to do. At night he expands. The walls cannot contain him. He moves throughout the world and he touches the stars.

"Ah," I thought, "poetry." To bring him down to earth I began to ask, "Well, during the day, in his REAL body . . ."

"Wait," he said, "that's the difference between us and you. You people regularly assume that the contracted state is the real body. It IS real, in a sense. But here we tend to start from the other end, the expanded state. The daytime state we refer to as the 'body of fear.' And whereas you tend to judge a monk by his decorum during the day, we tend to measure a monk by the number of persons he touches at night, and the number of stars."

Father Theophane

Knowing others is wisdom; knowing the self is enlightenment.

Tao Te Ching

A human being has so many skins inside, covering the depths of the heart. We know so many things, but we don't know ourselves! Why, thirty or forty skins or hides, as thick and hard as an ox's or a bear's, cover the soul. Go into your own ground and learn to know yourself there.

Meister Eckhart

God is not external to anyone, but is present with all things, though they are ignorant that He is so.

Plotinus

"Allah, how long have I been calling you and you have not revealed yourself?" From the depths of consciousness came a voice that said: "What do you think has been making you call on me all this time?"

Sufi

The Question

Said the monk, "All these mountains and rivers and the earth and stars— where do they come from?"
Said the master, "Where does your question come from?"

It does not matter what name you attach to it, but your consciousness must ascend to the point through which you view the universe with your God-centered nature. The feeling accompanying this experience is that of complete oneness with the Universal Whole. One merges into a euphoria of absolute unity with all life: with humanity, with all the creatures of the earth, the trees and plants, the air, the water, and even earth itself. This God-centered nature is constantly awaiting to govern your life gloriously. You have the free will to either allow it to govern your life, or not to allow it to affect you. This choice is always yours!

Peace Pilgrim

Consciousness

I do not see a delegation
For the Four-footed.
I see no seat for the eagles.
We forget and we consider
Ourselves superior.
But we are after all
A mere part of the Creation.

And we must consider
To understand where we are.

And we stand somewhere between
The mountain and the Ant.

Somewhere and only there
As part and parcel
Of the Creation.

Chief Oren Lyons, From an address to the Non-Governmental Organizations of the United Nations, Geneva, Switzerland, 1977

For now we see through a glass darkly; but then face to face; now I know in part; but then shall I know even as also I am known.

I Corinthians

On January 23rd, 1961, I came home after an evening lecture at the house of some friends. It was a freezing night . . . I had absolutely no premonitions of anything unusual, but suddenly, I don't know exactly what happened, but it was a bit like a long electric shock. Of course this was quite different, it wasn't mechanical, it was a person; I could have no doubt about this at all. There was a feeling of heat and light rushing through my bloodstream, sweeping over me and paralysing me almost, as if some person outside were blowing something in me to white heat, and I was sobbing tears of love and gratitude. I was longing for it to go on and for some time it kept returning more and more strongly, leaving me weak and shivering in between. There were no visions or voices, but the person communicated with words, or rather ideas, or certainties, with a sort of close intimacy, much more closely than into my ear or imagination . . . .

For more than a week I went about as if I were drunk; I could think of nothing else and spent a lot of time waiting and praying and hoping for more of this sensation for the sheer happiness of it. But it was always below the surface, like an electric heater unexpectedly being switched on at the most unlikely moments—such as driving on busy roads, in supermarkets, or walking about, gardening or doing housework.

Meg Maxwell and Verena Tschudin, *Seeing the Invisible*
from The Alister Hardy Research Center

Man is not alone
On the Chessboard of Life.
He is surrounded by Divine Powers,
Love and Wisdom,
and all the good forces of Providence
in this world of Shadows and Lights.

Tolstoy

Communion with the Angels

The Noon Peace Contemplations, dedicated each day to a different one of the seven aspects of Peace, were addressed to the Heavenly Father, requesting him to send the Angel of Peace to all, and then to send a certain one of the angels to strengthen each aspect of the Sevenfold Peace. The words follow:

Peace With the Body
Our Father who art in heaven,
send to all
your Angel of Peace;

to our body
the Angel of Life.

Peace With the Mind
Our Father who art in heaven,
send to all
your Angel of Peace;
to our mind the
Angel of Power.

Peace With the Family
Our Father who art in heaven,
send to all
Your Angel of Peace;
to our family and friends
the Angel of Love.

Peace With Humanity
Our Father who art in heaven,
send to all
Your Angel of Peace;
to humanity
the Angel of Work.

Peace With Culture
Our Father who art in heaven,
send to all
Your Angel of Peace;
to our knowledge,
the Angel of Wisdom.

Peace With the Kingdom of The Earthly Mother
Our Father who art in heaven,
send to all
Your Angel of Peace;
to the kingdom of our Earthly Mother,
the Angel of Joy.

Peace With the Kingdom of The Heavenly Father
Our Father who art in heaven,
send to all
Your Angel of Peace;
to Your Kingdom, our Heavenly Father,
Your Angel of Eternal Life.

Edmond Bordeaux Szekely,
The Teachings of the Essenes from Enoch to the Dead Sea Scrolls

❧❧❧❧❧❧❧❧❧

Why the Dog Could Not Drink

Shibli was asked:
'Who guided you in the Path?'
He said: 'A dog. One day I saw him, almost dead with thirst, standing by the water's edge.

'Every time he looked at his reflection in the water he was frightened, and withdrew, because he thought it was another dog.

'Finally, such was his necessity, he cast away fear and leapt into the water; at which the "other dog" vanished.

'The dog found that the obstacle, which was himself, the barrier between him and what he sought, melted away.

'In this same way my own obstacle vanished, when I knew that it was what I took to be my own self. And my Way was first shown to me by the behaviour of—a dog.'

❧❧❧❧❧❧❧❧❧

Most people live, whether physically, intellectually or morally, in a very restricted circle of their potential being. They make use of a very small portion of their possible consciousness, and of their soul's resources in general, much like a man who, out of his whole bodily organism, should get into a habit of using and moving only his little finger.

William James

❧❧❧❧❧❧❧❧❧

The Golden Eagle

A man found an eagle's egg and put it in the nest of a backyard hen. The eaglet hatched with the brood of chicks and grew up with them.

All his life the eagle did what the backyard chickens did, thinking he was a backyard chicken. He scratched the earth for worms and insects. He clucked and cackled. And he would thrash his wings and fly a few feet into the air.

Years passed and the eagle grew very old. One day he saw a magnificent bird far above him in the cloudless sky. It glided in graceful majesty among the powerful wind currents, with scarcely a beat of its strong golden wings.

The old eagle looked up in awe. "Who's that?" he asked.

"That's the eagle, the king of the birds," said his neighbor. "He belongs to the sky. We belong to the earth—we're chickens."

So the eagle lived and died a chicken, for that's what he thought he was.

❧❧❧❧❧❧❧❧❧

There was once a man who was very stupid. Each morning when he woke he had such a hard time finding his clothes that he almost feared to go to bed when he thought of the trouble he would have on waking.

One night he got himself a pencil and pad and jotted down the exact name and location of each item of clothing as he undressed. Next morning he pulled out his pad and read, "pants"—there they were. He stepped into them. "Shirt"—there it was. He pulled it over his head. "Hat"—there it was. He slapped it on his head.

He was very pleased about all this till a horrible thought struck him. "And I—where am I?" He had forgotten to jot that down. So he searched and searched, but in vain. He could not find himself.

❧❧❧❧❧❧❧❧❧

God expects but one thing of you, and that is that you should come out of yourself in so far as you are a created being and let God be God in you.

Meister Eckhart

❧❧❧❧❧❧❧❧❧

We can only learn to know ourselves and do what we can—namely, surrender our will and fulfill God's will in us.

Saint Teresa of Ávila

❧❧❧❧❧❧❧❧❧

If your heart were sincere and upright, every creature would be unto you a looking-glass of life and a book of holy doctrine.

Thomas à Kempis

❧❧❧❧❧❧❧❧❧

There is a spark of good in everybody, no matter how deeply it may be buried. *It is the real you.* When I say 'you' what am I really thinking of? Am I thinking of the clay garment, the body? No, that's not the real you. Am I thinking of the self-centered nature? No, that's not the real you. The real you is that divine spark. Some call this the God-centered nature, others the divine nature and the Kingdom of God within. Hindus know it as nirvana; the Buddhists refer to it as the awakened soul; the Quakers see it as the Inner Light. In other places it is known as the Christ in you, the Christ Consciousness, the hope of glory, or the indwelling spirit. Even some psychologists have a name for it, the superconscious. But it is all the same thing dressed in different words. The important thing to remember is that it dwells within you!

Peace Pilgrim

Know the Self as Lord of the chariot,
The body as the chariot itself,
The discriminating intellect as
The charioteer, and the mind as the reins.
The senses, say the wise, are the horses,
Selfish desires are the roads they travel.

Katha Upanishad

Lay not up for yourselves treasures upon earth, where moth and rust doth corrupt, and where thieves break through and steal:

But lay up for yourselves treasures in heaven, where neither moth nor rust doth corrupt, and where thieves do not break through nor steal:

For where your treasure is, there will your heart be also.

The light of the body is the eye: if therefore thine eye be single, thy whole body shall be full of light.

But if thine eye be evil, thy whole body shall be full of darkness. If therefore the light that is in thee be darkness, how great *is* that darkness!

No man can serve two masters: for either he will hate the one, and love the other; or else he will hold to the one, and despise the other. Ye cannot serve God and mammon.

Therefore I say unto you, Take no thought for your life, what ye shall eat, or what ye shall drink: nor yet for your body, what ye shall put on. Is not the life more than meat, and the body than raiment?

Behold the fowls of the air: for they sow not, neither do they reap, nor gather into barns; yet your heavenly Father feedeth them. Are ye not much better than they?

Which of you by taking thought can add one cubit unto his stature?

And why take ye thought for raiment? Consider the lilies of the field, how they grow; they toil not, neither do they spin:

And yet I say unto you, That even Solomon in all his glory was not arrayed like one of these.

Wherefore, if God so clothe the grass of the field, which to day is, and to morrow is cast into the oven, *shall* he not much more *clothe* you, O ye of little faith?

Therefore take no thought, saying, What shall we eat? or, What shall we drink? or, Wherewithal shall we be clothed?

(For after all these things do the Gentiles seek:) for your heavenly Father knoweth that ye have need of all these things.

But seek ye first the kingdom of God, and his righteousness: and all these things shall be added unto you.

Take therefore no thought for the morrow: for the morrow shall take thought for the things of itself. Sufficient unto the day *is* the evil thereof.

The Gospel According to Saint Matthew

What this little child would recommend for you is to sit under a tree. By tree I mean a real saint. A saint is like a tree. He does not call anyone, neither does he send anyone away. He gives shelter to whoever cares to come, be it a man, woman, child or an animal. If you sit under a tree it will protect you from the weather, from the scorching sun as well as from the pouring rain, and it will give you flowers and fruit. Whether a human being enjoys them or a bird tastes of them matters little to the tree; its produce is there for anyone who comes and takes it. And last but not least, it gives itself. How itself? The fruit contains the seeds for new trees of a similar kind. So, by sitting under a tree you will get shelter, shade, flowers, fruit, and in due course you will come to know your Self.

Anandamayi Ma, *As the Flower Sheds its Fragrance*

One of the most renowned sages in ancient India was Svetaketu. This is how he came by his wisdom. When he was no more than seven years of age, he was sent by his father to study the Vedas. By dint of application and intelligence, the lad outshone all his fellow students until in time he was considered the greatest living expert on the Scriptures—and this when he was barely past his youth.

On his return home his father wished to test the ability of his son. This is the question he put to him: "Have you learned that by learning which there is no need to learn anything else? Have you discovered that by discovering which all suffering ceases? Have you mastered that which cannot be taught?"

"No," said Svetaketu.

"Then," said his father, "what have you learned in all these years is worthless, my son."

So impressed was Svetaketu by the truth of his father's words that he set off to discover through silence the wisdom which cannot be expressed in words.

ટ&ટ&ટ&ટ&ટ&ટ&ટ&

In the first days of my youth, I tried to find it in the creatures, as I saw others do; but the more I sought, the less I found it, and the nearer I went to it, the further off it was. For of every image that appeared to me, before I had fully tested it, or abandoned myself to peace in it, an inner voice said to me: "This is not what thou seekest."

Heinrich Suso

ટ&ટ&ટ&ટ&ટ&ટ&ટ&

We are celebrating the feast of the Eternal Birth which God the Father has borne and never ceases to bear in all Eternity . . . . But if it takes not place in me, what avails it? Everything lies in this, that it should take place in me.

Meister Eckhart

ટ&ટ&ટ&ટ&ટ&ટ&ટ&

A Sophist approached one of the Wise Men of ancient Greece, and thought to puzzle him with the most perplexing questions. But the Sage of Miletus was equal to the test for he replied to them all, without the least hesitation yet with the utmost exactitude.

1.   What is the oldest of all things?
     "God, because He has always existed."

2.   What is the most beautiful of all things?
     "The Universe, because it is the work of God."

3.   What is the greatest of all things?
     "Space, because it contains all that has been created."

4.   What is the most constant of all things?
     "Hope, because it still remains with man, after he has lost everything else."

5.   What is the best of all things?
     "Virtue, because without it there is nothing good."

6.   What is the quickest of all things?
     "Thought, because in less than a minute it can fly to the end of the universe."

7. What is the strongest of all things?
    "Necessity, which makes man face all the dangers of life."

8. What is the easiest of all things?
    "To give Advice."

But when it came to the ninth question our sage pronounced a paradox. He gave an answer which I am certain his worldly wise querent never understood, and which to most people will give only the most superficial meaning.

The question was:

What is the most difficult of all things?

And the Miletian sage replied:

"To know Thyself."

This was the bidding to ignorant man from the ancient sages; this shall be the bidding yet.

Retold by Paul Brunton, *The Secret Path*

౿ఎ౿ఎ౿ఎ౿ఎ౿ఎ౿ఎ

When I was a child, I spake as a child, I understood as a child, I thought as a child: but when I became a man I put away childish things.

I Corinthians

౿ఎ౿ఎ౿ఎ౿ఎ౿ఎ౿ఎ

As human beings, our greatness lies not so much in being able to remake the world—that is the myth of the "atomic age"—as in being able to remake ourselves.

Mahatma Gandhi

౿ఎ౿ఎ౿ఎ౿ఎ౿ఎ౿ఎ

A lad from Sienna snared in a birdtrap a big flock of doves and was carrying them all off alive to sell. But Saint Francis, who was always full of love and especially towards domestic animals and [wondrously] compassionate towards birds, seeing these doves, and moved with love and pity, said to the boy who was carrying them: "Good lad, I beg you, do hand over those doves to me, so that such innocent birds, which in the Bible are the symbols of pure, humble and faithful souls, may not fall into the hands of cruel people who will kill them." Inspired by God, the boy immediately handed them all over to Saint Francis. The holy father took them into his arms and began speaking to them. Sweetly he began to speak to them: "My sister doves, pure and innocent, why did you let yourselves be trapped? I want to rescue you from death, and make you nests, so that you may be fruitful and fulfill your Creator's commandment to multiply." Off went Francis and made a dovecote for them all.

The doves, taking up their nests built by Saint Francis, laid eggs and grew in number among the friars, and showed such friendship to the saint and the brothers, that they seemed like the hens which the brothers kept. They never went out without Saint Francis' blessing and permission. He said to the lad who gave him the doves: "Son, someday you will be a friar minor in this Order, and gracefully serve the Lord Jesus Christ." And so it fell out. He entered the Order and lived a commendable and exemplary life to the end, thanks to the merits of the holy father. To the praise of our Lord Jesus Christ. Amen.

ð ð ð ð ð ð ð

Man's heart strives after unending eternal happiness. Thou hast created us, O Lord, for Thyself and our heart is restless until it rests in Thee.

Saint Augustine

ð ð ð ð ð ð ð

This is certain, and I would often remember how when a storm arose on the sea, the Lord commanded the winds to be still. Then I would say to myself: 'Who is this whom all my faculties thus obey? Who is it that in a moment sheds light amidst such great darkness, who softens a heart that seemed to be of stone and sheds the water of gentle tears where for so long it had seemed to be dry? Who gives these desires? Who gives this courage? What have I been thinking of? What am I afraid of? What is this? I wish to serve this Lord, and have no other aim but to please Him. I seek no contentment, no rest, no other blessing but to do His will.' I seemed to feel so confident of this that I could affirm it.

Saint Teresa of Ávila

ð ð ð ð ð ð ð

Try to treat with equal love all the people
with whom you have relations. Thus
the abyss between 'myself' and 'yourself'
will be filled in, which is the goal of
all religious worship.

Anandamayi Ma

❧❧❧❧❧❧

A human being is part of the whole, called by us "universe," a part limited in time and space. He experiences himself, his thoughts and feelings, as something separate from the rest—a kind of optical delusion of consciousness. This delusion is a kind of prison for us, restricting us to our personal desires and to affection for a few persons nearest to us. Our task must be to free ourselves from this prison by widening our circle of compassion to embrace all living creatures and the whole of nature in its beauty.

Albert Einstein

❧❧❧❧❧❧

The surest way to live with honor in the world is to be in reality what we appear to be.

Socrates

❧❧❧❧❧❧

The spirit of man is the candle of the Lord.

Proverbs

❧❧❧❧❧❧

Part II

Lighting the Divine Fire

Lighting the Divine Fire

Amma Syncletica said: In the beginning, there is struggle and a lot of work for those who come near to God. But after that, there is indescribable joy. It is just like building a fire: at first it's smoky and your eyes water, but later you get the desired result. Thus we ought to light the divine fire in ourselves with tears and effort.

Desert Fathers

Once upon a crossroad, Joy and Sorrow met, then gathered around the fireside to tell tales of their wanderings. "Why are you here?" each asked the other. "Where have you been? What do you seek?" Sorrow spoke eloquently about the dust along the road, stormy days, and the bitter tears and fears of life. Joy said nothing is simply itself—the world is a love song from the divine Source of life while the heart is, in its depths, a sanctuary of silence entered through prayer.

Joy and Sorrow met at the crossroad, each seeking the summit of the Holy Mountain. They came from different directions, but there was no difference between them. Some seek in pain; others in prayer. Yet they are inseparable, each the face of the other. To approach the Holy Mountain of Truth, we begin where we are, as we are. The mysteries of Love ask not that we make a desperate attempt to "be good," but that we begin a gentle, honest effort to grow through the disciplines of realization. Just as the flower does not force itself to bloom, the tree of our soul, in its own natural rhythm, unfolds its branches to bear the fruit of the heart.

Joy and Sorrow met at the crossroad, each perceiving the spirit of the other, each yearning "to light the divine fire" within themselves. Generations of pilgrims on the quest have followed their spiritual traditions to the Holy Mountain. From all directions they have come in both pain and prayer, joy and sorrow to build a fire with "tears and effort."

"The divine fire" is a poem of nature—our true nature—which leaves its footprints everywhere. To follow the trail of light, in our own unique way, initiates a new way of seeing as though observing for the first time that when we look in a mirror we see ourselves, not the state of the mirror. The container is not the contained; the fire is not its Creator. Such a shift in awareness intensifies the longing to scale the highest peaks of consciousness en route Home. But today, far from the roads of yesterday, we struggle to "light the divine fire:" we chop wood, create a clearing, build a fire, and open our tear-stained eyes to dancing flames of light.

In *Letting Go*, we discover stories—of simplicity, obstacles, faith, attachments, the real—which point arrows into our inner lives, penetrating the masks we wear in the world. As Teilhard de Chardin says, "We are not human beings having a spiritual experience. We are spiritual beings having a human experience." Have we forgotten who we are? Our spiritual heritage and destiny are hidden in the midst of memory ready to awaken. But lodged around our hearts are opinions, beliefs, cravings, preoccupations with the past, yearnings for the future, patterns of self-protection. They are like stones cast in the clear pond of consciousness, creating ripples which conceal the deeper rhythms. The disciplines of realization reveal "heartstones" for what they are and have us listen to the ageless ring of truth which calls us away from that which distracts us— what was, what might be—to That which Is. We are summoned to the present moment by a timeless sound, to a life of faith and simplicity.

Simplicity, however, is not deprivation. It is not what we have that binds us but what we hold on to in a desperate attempt to hide from our fear of loss. We tie up our heart when we become possessed by our accumulations, accomplishments, and desires for more. Gandhi said "there is enough in the world for everyone's need, but not for everyone's greed."

True simplicity is a state of the heart. We do not hold on to what is passing but fully appreciate each moment as a gift. With an open heart, we embrace each sunset, every rainstorm, all gentle caresses of the wind and are moved to greater compassion beyond our personal world. No longer a stagnant marshland of attachments, we are a flowing river singing its way into the secrets of the sea. Scattered diversions flee the light. Fears are transformed into trust. We are opened to new seasons of love and laughter, creativity and understanding.

Beyond simplicity, we discover that everyday obstacles are opportunities for spiritual growth in disguise. We penetrate veils of confusion as we experience the distinctions between wise and immature faith. Wise faith gives us courage to explore beyond the horizon to unknown realms, to question, to learn from challenges. Immature faith has the potential for intolerance, narrowness, and blind obedience. Wise faith is a compassionate teacher without judgment or malice while an immature faith acts as an appointed custodian of spiritual mysteries. To be wise is not only to learn from others but also to be a lamp unto ourselves wherein we do not forsake the light of our inner truth.

A wise faith encourages us to move beyond our attachment to anger, worry, fear, and greed; to make our energy available for service to a more harmonious way of being. Rather than chasing after emotional experiences or flailing through a sea of anger, we enter deeper channels of compassion for ourselves and others. In the process, we learn to "love the Dandelions" of our life; our heart swings wide open to include all in its path.

In *Letting Go*, we discover that contentment is not possessiveness but a wise and loving heart; that the spiritual journey requires great faith and common sense. What do we hold on to as a way to protect ourselves from fear? How is our life more complex than simple? What anger or fear is lodged around our heart awaiting release? What tests of life are creating greater depths of compassion? What opens our heart to the present moment?

In *Training the Heart and Mind*, we discover stories which embody love and wisdom, that call us from the shores of knowledge into the depths of eternity's secrets. Before knowledge and reality meet, however, knowledge remains cooped up in the dark. After the candleflame of light illuminates the darkness, knowledge is quiet, rapt in awe at the harmony of natural and cosmic law. In the fabric of our being, we are all connected; every particle lives in the luster of light.

As Jesus said in the *Gospel of Saint Thomas*, "I am the light that shines over everything. I am the All. From me the all came forth, and to me the all has returned. Split a piece of wood, and I am there. Pick up a stone, and you will find me there." True knowledge is an expression of the All made visible in the spirit of life. It cannot be divorced from love and respect for the dignity of all that lives.

In *Training the Heart and Mind* we read stories which are a living expression of spirituality, stories which highlight the changing rhythm of our inner life as we experience the wilderness, oasis, and deserts of consciousness.

Through prayer and meditation we traverse through the changing landscape of consciousness to That which lives in our deepest center. It is love, however, that stirs us to enter this cloud of unknowing in our naked attempt toward God. Then in the deep silence of the spirit are born peace, wisdom, and wholeness. We learn to embrace the joys and sorrows of life. Once impatient with questions, we learn to love the questions themselves.

In its essence, prayer is love for God, and the spiritual journey is training in love. With each gate that opens to us—the desire to know God, purification and unfoldment, atonement, acts of devotion, certainty, love for God, unity—our self-centered nature, or self-will, shows itself for a time, basking in the fruits of its own endeavors. But it is not the ego which has freed us. It is God who keeps us in a state of love. All is God; all is His; all by Him. Eventually, we only desire what God desires; we live in peace and joy in both worlds.

Each step of the pilgrim's way is training in love. Our responsibility is to live according to the highest light we have, to seek what is Real in a sea of impermanence. The hallmark of the spiritual journey is expressed, in Christianity, in the first commandment: to love God above all else. It is expressed in the world as a loving embrace for all that lives.

Love is a brilliant coat of many colors. It is forgiveness, humility, service, the revelation of unknown depths of the mind. It is an open heart which seeks direction from one experienced in the path *to* God and life *with* God. Love seeks not to blame nor judge, to flatter nor diminish another. It is Friend to all. No shadow can withstand the dazzling light of love; all is transformed in its presence.

The stories in *Training the Heart and Mind* reveal the integrity of the spiritual journey and the development of character that accompanies growth in love. But the chapter title is an artificial distinction, a play on words. The

Chinese have only one word for heart and mind, and it symbolizes the reality of Self which knows neither birth nor death. In the *Gospel of Saint Thomas*, Jesus said, "If your teachers say to you, 'Look, the kingdom is in heaven,' then the birds will get there before you. But the kingdom is inside you, and it is outside you. If you know yourselves, then you will be known; and you will know that you are the sons [daughters] of the living Father."

It is for each of us to "build the divine fire within ourselves," to experience the silence which chants hymns of peace and discloses the secrets of eternity.

As pilgrims along the way, we gently embrace the lessons of love. Who can we love today? What is our heart open to this moment? What do we need to forgive in ourselves and others? How do we wish to be treated when we make mistakes? How can we see to new depths of humility, forgiveness, and tolerance? What is our central focus of life, that to which we give our greatest love?

Chapter I

Letting Go

Pray for a Contented Mind

The Lord Vishnu said to his devotee: "I am weary of your constant petitions. I have decided to grant you any three things you ask for. After that, I shall give you nothing more."

The devotee delightedly made his first petition at once. He asked that his wife should die so that he could marry a better woman. His petition was immediately granted.

But when friends and relatives gathered for the funeral and began to recall all the good qualities of his wife, the devotee realized he had been hasty. He now realized he had been blind to all her virtues. Was he likely to find another woman as good as her?

So he asked the Lord to bring her back to life! That left him with just one petition. He was determined not to make a mistake this time, for he would have no chance to correct it. He consulted widely. Some of his friends advised him to ask for immortality. But of what good was immortality, said others, if he did not have good health? And of what use was health if he had no money? And of what use was money if he had no friends?

Years passed and he could not make up his mind what to ask for: life or health or wealth or power or love. Finally he said to the Lord, "Please advise me on what to ask for."

The Lord laughed when he saw the man's predicament, and said, "Ask to be content no matter what you get."

He is not elated by good fortune or depressed by bad. His mind is established in God, and he is free from delusion.

Sri Krishna, *Bhagavad Gita*

On the one hand I felt the call of God; on the other, I continued to follow the world. All the things of God gave me great pleasure, but I was held captive by those of the world. I might have been said to be trying to reconcile these two extremes, to bring contraries together: the spiritual life on the one hand and worldly satisfactions, pleasures, and pastimes on the other.

Saint Teresa of Ávila

It is permissible to take life's blessings with both hands provided thou dost know thyself prepared in the opposite event to take them just as gladly. This applies to food and friends and kindred, to anything God gives and takes away . . . . As long as God is satisfied do thou rest content. If He is pleased to want something else of thee, still rest content.

Meister Eckhart

Remember, no human condition is ever permanent; then you will not be overjoyed in good fortune, nor too sorrowful in misfortune.

Socrates

Let go. Why cling to the pain and the wrongs of yesterday? Why hold on to the very things that keep you from hope and love?

Buddha

The poor man had come to the end of his rope. So he went to his rabbi for advice.

"Holy Rabbi!" he cried. "Things are in a bad way with me, and are getting worse all the time! We are poor, so poor, that my wife, my six children, my in-laws, and I have to live in a one-room hut. We get in each other's way all the time. Our nerves are frayed, and, because we have plenty of troubles, we quarrel. Believe me—my home is a hell and I'd sooner die than continue living this way!"

The rabbi pondered the matter gravely. "My son," he said, "promise to do as I tell you and your condition will improve."

"I promise, Rabbi," answered the troubled man. "I'll do anything you say."

"Tell me—what animals do you own?"

"I have a cow, a goat, and some chickens."

"Very well! Go home now and take all these animals into your house to live with you."

The poor man was dumbfounded, but since he had promised the rabbi, he went home and brought all the animals into his house.

The following day the poor man returned to the rabbi and cried, "Rabbi, what a misfortune have you brought upon me! I did as you told me and brought the animals into the house. And now what have I got? Things are worse than ever! My life is a perfect hell—the house is turned into a barn! Save me, Rabbi—help me!"

"My son," replied the rabbi serenely, "go home and take the chickens out of your house. God will help you!"

So the poor man went home and took the chickens out of his house. But it was not long before he again came running to the rabbi.

"Holy Rabbi!" he wailed. "Help me, save me! The goat is smashing every-thing in the house—she's turning my life into a nightmare."

"Go home," said the rabbi gently, "and take the goat out of the house. God will help you!"

The poor man returned to his house and removed the goat. But it wasn't long before he again came running to the rabbi, lamenting loudly, "What a misfortune you've brought upon my head, Rabbi! The cow has turned my house into a stable! How can you expect a human being to live side by side with an animal?"

"You're right—a hundred times right!" agreed the rabbi. "Go straight home and take the cow out of your house!"

And the poor unfortunate hastened home and took the cow out of his house.

Not a day had passed before he came running again to the rabbi.

"Rabbi!" cried the poor man, his face beaming. "You've made life sweet again for me. With all the animals out, the house is so quiet, so roomy, and so clean! What a pleasure!"

Chassid

A Brother of St. Francis

When I told the guestmaster I was a Brother of St. Francis, he promptly asked me to come and tell the community about St. Francis. When I agreed, he seemed very pleased and went right out to ring the great bell. They came in by the hundreds, monks and nuns, and sat down on the floor. As soon as the guestmaster announced that I was a Brother of St. Francis, a buzz of excitement swept the room. In fact, so obvious was their delight, that I asked them how they had come to be so interested in St. Francis. A sprightly old nun stood up and said. "Why, he was here, didn't you know?" With the broadest of smiles she continued, "We invited him once to make our visitation." I was sure she was pulling my leg. "That man he did us so much good."

Then they began to tell me the beautiful things he said—and the funny things. They laughed and laughed. Then someone got up to show me how he danced. Soon they were all up, singing and dancing. All became quiet when an old monk started to tell how Brother Francis had spoken to them of the Passion of Christ, holding up his hand for all to see the wound. We wept, all of us. After a while I became aware that they had stopped, but I, I could not stop weeping. Then one by one they came, embraced me, and whispered, "Peace, Brother." Every last one of them came.

Father Theophane

Flow with whatever may happen and let your mind be free. Stay centered by accepting whatever you are doing. This is the ultimate.

Chuang Tsu

SIMPLICITY IS FREEDOM

One is rich not through one's possessions, but through that which one can with dignity do without.

Epicurus

Possessions

You possess only whatever will not be lost in a shipwreck.

Sufi

God Made Everything so Simple

"God made everything so simple. Our lives are very simple. We do what we please. The only law we obey is the natural law, God's law. We abide only by that. We don't need your church. We have the Black Hills for our church. And we don't need your Bible. We have the wind and the rain and the stars for our Bible. The world is an open Bible for us. We Indians have studied it for millions and millions of years.

We've learned that God rules the universe and that everything God made is living. Even the rocks are alive. When we use them in our sweat ceremony we talk to them and they talk back to us."

Mathew King/Native American Elder/Lakota

Driven by fear, people run for security to mountains and forests, to sacred spots and shrines. But none of these can be a safe refuge, because they cannot free the mind from fear.

Dhammapada

Give up anger, give up pride, and free yourself from worldly bondage. No sorrow can befall those who never try to possess people and things as their own.

Dhammapada

I'll tell you about one more woman. She was liberated, although not in the best possible way. I saw her only occasionally, but I happened to see her about a month after her huge house, in which she and her husband had been living alone since the children were grown, had burned down while they'd been out. They lost everything except the clothes they were wearing. Remembering how attached she had been to that huge house, in spite of the fact that it was such a burden for her to take care of, I started to say a few words of sympathy. But she said, "Don't sympathize with me! Now, you could have the morning after, but not now. Just think, I will never have to clean out that attic. I will never have to clean out those clothes closets. I will never have to clean that basement! Why, I've never felt so free. I just feel I'm starting life all over again!"

Peace Pilgrim

Death comes and carries off a man absorbed in his family and possessions as the monsoon flood sweeps away a sleeping village.

Dhammapada

The more we have the less we own.

Meister Eckhart

Socrates believed that the wise person would instinctively lead a frugal life, and he even went so far as to refuse to wear shoes. Yet he constantly fell under the spell of the marketplace and would go there often to look at the great variety and magnificence of the wares on display.

A friend once asked him why he was so intrigued with the allures of the market. "I love to go there," Socrates replied, "to discover how many things I am perfectly happy without."

Conquer anger through gentleness, unkindness through kindness, greed through generosity, and falsehood by truth. Be truthful; do not yield to anger. Give freely, even if you have but little. The gods will bless you.

Dhammapada

꿍꿍꿍꿍꿍

A blackbird found a large piece of food in the village and lit out into the sky with the food in its beak. A flock of his brothers chased after him and raucously attacked the food, pulling it from his beak. The blackbird finally let go of the last piece and the frenzied flock left him alone. The bird swooped and dived and thought, "I have lost the food but I have regained the peaceful sky."

Sufi

꿍꿍꿍꿍꿍

OBSTACLES AND OPPORTUNITIES

꿍꿍꿍꿍꿍

Salt and Cotton in the River

Nasrudin was taking a load of salt to the market. His donkey waded through the river and the salt dissolved. When it reached the opposite bank the animal ran around in circles, overjoyed that its load had been lightened. Nasrudin was annoyed.

On the next market day he packed the panniers with cotton. The ass nearly drowned with the increased weight of the cotton soaked in river water.

"There!" said Nasrudin gleefully. "That will teach you to think that each time you go through water you stand to gain!"

Sufi

꿍꿍꿍꿍꿍

Long ago, the People had no light. It was hard for them to move around in the darkness and they were always cold. Mink took pity on them. He heard that on the other side of the world there was something called the Sun. It was being kept there by those on the other side of the world. So Mink decided to steal the Sun for the People. It was not an easy job, but Mink was a great thief. He stole the Sun and placed it in the sky so that it would share its light equally with the People on both sides of the world. Now it was no longer dark and cold all the time. Now there was day and night because of the Sun. The People were very happy and they praised Mink. He grew proud of himself because of that praise.

"Perhaps," he said, "there is something else I can steal for the People."

A long time passed and Mink saw nothing that was worth stealing. Then the Europeans came. They were new people with a lot of power.

"What is it that these new people have that we do not have?" Mink said.

Then he saw what it was. The Europeans had something they called Time. They used it to give them their power. So Mink decided he would steal Time. He waited until it was dark and sneaked into their house. There, in the biggest room, they kept Time up on a shelf. They kept it in a shiny box which made noises. As it made noises, two small arrows on the front of that box moved in circles. Mink could see it was a powerful thing. So he carried it off.

Now Mink and the People had Time. But Mink soon found that it was not easy to have Time. He had to watch the hands of that shiny box all of the time to see what the time was. He had to keep three keys tied around his neck so that he could use them to wind up that box full of time so it would keep on ticking. Now that Mink had Time, he no longer had the time to do the things he used to do. There was no time for him to fish and hunt as he had done before. He had to get up at a certain time and go to bed at a certain time. He had to go to meetings and work when the box full of Time told him it was time. He and the People were no longer free.

Because Mink stole Time, it now owned him and the People. It has been that way ever since then. Time owns us the way we used to own the Sun.

Native American

The Problem is Heaviness

Let me tell you something that happened on the last day of my retreat. I told the guestmaster that I didn't think I'd be able to get back soon because I wouldn't have the time. He came right back with "The problem is not TIME; the problem is HEAVINESS."

He turned and went downstairs, returning with a little carpet. "Here, take this. It is a magic carpet. If you'll just sit on it and let go of your heaviness, you can go anywhere you want. It's not a question of time."

I have come to know that this is true. People laugh at me when I tell them. Will you laugh too? All right. Then stay there.

Father Theophane

This, Too, Will Pass

A powerful king, ruler of many domains, was in a position of such magnificence that wise men were his mere employees. And yet one day he felt himself confused and called the sages to him.

He said:

'I do not know the cause, but something impels me to seek a certain ring, one that will enable me to stabilize my state.

'I must have such a ring. And this ring must be one which, when I am unhappy, will make me joyful. At the same time, if I am happy and look upon it, I must be made sad.'

The wise men consulted one another, and threw themselves into deep contemplation, and finally they came to a decision as to the character of this ring which would suit their king.

The ring which they devised was one upon which was inscribed the legend:

THIS, TOO, WILL PASS

Sufi

There is a story of the great Tibetan teacher Marpa, who lived on a farm with his family a thousand years ago in Tibet. On the farm, there also lived many monks who came to study with this great teacher. One day Marpa's oldest son was killed. Marpa was grieving deeply when one of the monks came to him and said, "I don't understand. You teach us that all is an illusion. Yet you are crying. If all is an illusion, then why do you grieve so deeply?" Marpa replied, "Indeed, everything is an illusion. And the death of a child is the greatest of these illusions."

Buddhist

During his first visit to England, a great Master from Thailand, Achaan Chah spoke to many Buddhist groups. One evening after a talk he received a question from a dignified English lady who had spent many years studying the complex cybernetics of the mind according to the eighty-nine classes of consciousness in the Buddhist abhidharma psychology texts. Would he please explain certain of the more difficult aspects of this system of psychology to her so she could continue her study?

Buddhism teaches us to let go. But at first, we naturally cling to the principles of Buddhism. The wise person takes these principles and uses them as tools to discover the essence of our life. Sensing how caught up she was in intellectual concepts rather than benefiting from practice in her own heart, Achaan Chah answered her quite directly, "You, madam, are like one who keeps hens in her yard," he told her, "and goes around picking up the chicken droppings instead of the eggs."

Buddhist

Cut down the whole forest of selfish desires, not just one tree only. Cut down the whole forest and you will be on your way to liberation.

Dhammapada

As fresh milk needs time to curdle, a selfish deed takes time to bring sorrow in its wake. Like fire smoldering under the ashes, slowly does it burn the immature.

Dhammapada

Bones to Test our Faith

A Christian scholar who held the Bible to be literally true was once accosted by a scientist who said, "According to the Bible the earth was created some five thousand years ago. But we have discovered bones that point to life on earth a million years ago."

Pat came the answer: "When God created earth five thousand years ago, he deliberately put those bones in to test our faith and see if we would believe his Word rather than scientific evidence."

Eat No Stones

A hunter, walking through some woods, came upon a notice. He read the words:

STONE-EATING IS FORBIDDEN

His curiosity was stimulated, and he followed a track which led past the sign until he came to a cave at the entrance to which a Sufi was sitting.

The Sufi said to him:

"The answer to your question is that you have never seen a notice prohibiting the eating of stones because there is no need for one. Not to eat stones may be called a common habit.

"Only when the human being is able similarly to avoid other habits, even more destructive than eating stones, will he be able to get beyond his present pitiful state."

First let us discuss a poor man as one who wants nothing. There are some . . . who do not understand this well. They are those who are attached to their own penances and external exercises . . . . God help those who hold divine truth in such low esteem! Such people present an outward picture that gives them the name of saints; but inside they are donkeys, for they cannot distinguish divine truth . . . . So I say that a man ought to be established, free and empty, not knowing or perceiving that God is acting in him; and so a man may possess poverty.

Meister Eckhart

Excuses

"Why not?" that was the first thing he said. He had never seen me before. I hadn't said a word. "Why not?" I knew he had me.

I brought up excuses: "My wife . . . the people I have to work with . . . not enough time . . . I guess it's my temperament . . . "

There was a sword hanging on the wall. He took it and gave it to me. "Here, with this sword, you can cut through any barriers." I took it and slipped away without saying a word.

Back in my room in the guesthouse I sat down and kept looking at that sword. I knew that what he said was true.

But the next day I returned his sword. How can I live without my excuses?

Father Theophane

Around the bones is built a house, plastered over with flesh and blood, in which dwell pride and pretence, old age and death. Even the chariot of a king loses its glitter in the course of time; so too the body loses its health and strength. But goodness does not grow old with the passage of time.

Dhammapada

On the day the Baal Shem Tov was dying, he called together his disciples and assigned each of them a task to carry on in his name, to continue his work. When he finished, he had still one more task. And so he called the last disciple and gave him this responsibility: to go all over Europe to retell stories about the Master. The disciple was very disappointed. This was hardly a prestigious job. But the Baal Shem Tov told him that he would not have to do this forever; he would receive a sign when he should stop and then he could live out the rest of his life in ease.

So after the Baal Shem Tov died, the disciple set off, and days and months turned into years and years of telling stories, until he felt he had told them in every part of the world. Then he heard of a man in Italy, a nobleman in fact, who would pay a gold ducat for each new story told. So the disciple made his way to Italy to the nobleman's castle. When he arrived, however, he discovered to his absolute horror that he had forgotten all the Baal Shem Tov stories! He couldn't remember a single one! He was mortified. But the nobleman was kind and urged him to stay on a few days anyway, in the hope that he would eventually remember something.

But the next day and again the next he remembered nothing. Finally, on the fourth day the disciple protested that he must go, out of sheer embarrassment. As he was about to leave, indeed as he was walking down the path leading from the nobleman's castle, suddenly he remembered one story. It wasn't much of a story, but at least it would prove that he was not a charlatan, that he indeed did know the great Baal Shem Tov, for he was the only disciple there when this story took place. Clinging to his memory of the story's thread, he made his way back to the castle, and as soon as he was shown into the nobleman's presence, this is the story the disciple began to pour out.

Once the Baal Shem Tov told him to harness the horses, so that they could take a trip to Turkey, where at this time of the year the streets were decorated for the Christians' Easter festival. The disciple was upset: It was well known that Jews were not safe in that part of Turkey during the Christian Holy Week and Easter. They were fair game for Christians shouting, "God-killer!" And, in fact, in the very region to which the Baal Shem Tov proposed to go, it was the custom during the Easter festival each year to kill one Jew in reparation.

Still, the Baal Shem Tov insisted and so they went. They went into the city and made their way into the Jewish quarter, where the Jews were all huddled indoors, behind closed shutters, out of fear. Thus secluded, they awaited the end of the festival, when they could go out on the streets again in safety. Imagine, then, how startled they were when the Baal Shem Tov, on being shown into the room where they were gathered, strode over to the shutters, threw them open, and stood there in full view, just as the procession was entering the town square!

Looking through the window, he saw the bishop leading the procession. The bishop was arrayed like a prince with gold vestments, silver mitre, and a diamond-studded staff. Turning to the disciple, the Baal Shem Tov said: "Go tell the bishop I want to see him." Was he out of his mind? Did he want to die? Did he want me to die? the disciple remembered wondering. But nothing could deter this order, so the disciple went out into the square and, making his way through the crowd, came around behind the bishop just as he was about to mount the platform to begin his sermon. More gesturing than speaking the words, the disciple hoarsely whispered to the bishop that the Baal Shem Tov wanted to see him.

The bishop seemed agitated and hesitated for a moment. But after his sermon, he came, and he and the Baal Shem Tov went immediately into a back room, where they were secluded together for three hours. Then the Master came out and, without saying anything else, told his disciple that they were ready to go back home.

As the disciple finished the story, he was about to apologize to the nobleman for its insignificance, for its lack of point, when he suddenly noticed the enormous impact the story had had on the nobleman. He had dissolved into tears and, finally, when he could speak, he said, "Oh, disciple, your story has just saved my soul! You see, I was there that day. I was that bishop. I had descended from a long line of distinguished rabbis but one day during a period of great persecution, I had abandoned the faith and converted to Christianity. The Christians, of course, were so pleased that, in time, they even made me a bishop. And I had accepted everything, even went along with the killing of the Jews each year until that one year. The night before the festival I had a terrible dream of the Day of Judgment and the danger to my soul. So when you came the very next day with a message from the Baal Shem Tov, I knew that I had to go to him.

"For three hours he and I talked. He told me that there still might be hope for my soul. He told me to sell my goods and retire on what was left and live a life of good deeds and holiness. There might still be hope. And his last words to me were these: 'When a man comes to you and tells you your own story, you will know that your sins are forgiven.' "

"So I have been asking everyone I knew for stories from the Baal Shem Tov. And I recognized you immediately when you came, and I was happy. But when I saw that all the stories had been taken from you, I recognized God's judgment. Yet now you have remembered one story, my story, and I know now that the Baal Shem Tov has interceded on my behalf and that God has forgiven me."

When a man comes to you and tells you your own story, you know that your sins are forgiven. And when you are forgiven, you are healed.

Hassidic Judaism

The Pharisee

When God walked into heaven and found that everyone was there, he wasn't pleased at all. He owed it to his justice, did he not, to carry out his threats. So everyone was summoned to his throne and the angel asked to read the Ten Commandments.

The first commandment was announced. Said God, "All who have broken this commandment will now betake themselves to hell." And so it was done.

The same was done with each of the commandments. By the time the angel came to read the seventh, no one was left in heaven except a recluse—smug and self-complacent.

God looked up and thought, "Only one person left in heaven? That makes it very lonesome." So he shouted out, "Come back, everyone!"

When the recluse heard that everyone was forgiven, he yelled in rage, "This is unjust! Why didn't you tell me this before?"

❧❧❧❧❧❧❧

FAITH OR DELUSION

❧❧❧❧❧❧❧

We always hope; and in all things it is better to hope than to despair. When we return to real trust in God, there will no longer be room in our soul for fear.

Goethe

❧❧❧❧❧❧❧

An atheist fell off a cliff. As he tumbled downward, he caught hold of the branch of a small tree. There he hung between heaven above and the rocks a thousand feet below, knowing he wasn't going to be able to hold on much longer.

Then an idea came to him. "God!" he shouted with all his might.

Silence! No one responded.

"God!" he shouted again. "If you exist, save me and I promise I shall believe in you and teach others to believe."

Silence again! Then he almost let go of the branch in shock as he heard a mighty Voice booming across the canyon. "That's what they all say when they are in trouble."

"No, God, No!" he shouted out, more hopeful now. "I am not like the others. Why, I have already begun to believe, don't you see, having heard your Voice for myself. Now all you have to do is save me and I shall proclaim your name to the ends of the earth."

"Very well," said the Voice. "I shall save you. Let go of that branch."

"Let go of the branch?" yelled the distraught man. "Do you think I'm crazy?"

❧❧❧❧❧❧❧

Mulla Nasrudin's house was on fire, so he ran up to his roof for safety.

There he was, precariously perched on the roof, when his friends gathered in the street below holding a stretched-out blanket for him and shouting, "Jump, Mulla, jump!"

"Oh no I won't," said the Mulla. "I know you fellows. If I jump, you'll pull the blanket away just to make a fool of me!"

"Don't be silly, Mulla. This isn't a joke. This is serious. Jump!"

"No," said Nasrudin. "I don't trust any of you. Lay that blanket on the ground and I'll jump."

Sufi

A priest was sitting at his desk by the window composing a sermon on providence when he heard something that sounded like an explosion. Soon he saw people running to and fro in a panic and discovered that a dam had burst, the river was flooding, and the people were being evacuated.

The priest saw the water begin to rise in the street below. He had some difficulty suppressing his own rising sense of panic, but he said to himself, "Here I am preparing a sermon on providence and I am being given an occasion to practice what I preach. I shall not flee with the rest. I shall stay right here and trust in the providence of God to save me."

By the time the water reached his window, a boat full of people came by. "Jump in, Father," they shouted. "Ah no, my children," said Father confidently. "I trust in the providence of God to save me."

Father did climb to the roof, however, and when the water got up there another boatload of people went by, urging Father to join them. Again he refused.

This time he climbed to the top of the belfry. When the water came up to his knees, an officer in a motorboat was sent to rescue him. "No thank you, officer," said Father, with a calm smile. "I trust in God, you see. He will never let me down."

When Father drowned and went to heaven, the first thing he did was complain to God. "I trusted you! Why did you do nothing to save me?"

"Well," said God. "I did send three boats, you know."

A disciple came riding on his camel to the tent of his Sufi Master. He dismounted and walked right into the tent, bowed low and said, "So great is my trust in God that I have left my camel outside untied, convinced that God protects the interests of those who love him."

"Go tie your camel, you fool!" said the Master. "God cannot be bothered doing for you what you are perfectly capable of doing for yourself."

Sufi

꧁꧂꧁꧂꧁꧂꧁꧂

A man walking through the forest saw a fox that had lost its legs and wondered how it lived. Then he saw a tiger come in with game in its mouth. The tiger had its fill and left the rest of the meat for the fox.

The next day God fed the fox by means of the same tiger. The man began to wonder at God's greatness and said to himself, "I too shall just rest in a corner with full trust in the Lord and he will provide me with all I need."

He did this for many days but nothing happened, and he was almost at death's door when he heard a voice say, "O you who are in the path of error, open your eyes to the truth! Follow the example of the tiger and stop imitating the disabled fox."

Sufi

꧁꧂꧁꧂꧁꧂꧁꧂

When the guru sat down to worship each evening, the ashram cat would get in the way and distract the worshipers. So he ordered that the cat be tied during evening worship.

After the guru died the cat continued to be tied during evening worship. And when the cat expired, another cat was brought to the ashram so that it could be duly tied during evening worship.

Centuries later learned treatises were written by the guru's scholarly disciples on the liturgical significance of tying up a cat while worship is performed.

Hindu

꧁꧂꧁꧂꧁꧂꧁꧂

A certain man caught a bird in a trap. The bird says, "Sir, you have eaten many cows and sheep in your life, and you're still hungry. The little bit of meat on my bones won't satisfy you either. If you let me go, I'll give you three pieces of wisdom. One I'll say standing on your hand. One on your roof. And one I'll speak from the limb of the tree."

The man was interested. He freed the bird and let it stand on his hand.

"Number One: Do not believe an absurdity, no matter who says it."

The bird flew and lit on the man's roof. "Number Two: Do not grieve over what is past. It's over. Never regret what has happened."

"By the way," the bird continued, "in my body there's a huge pearl weighing as much as ten copper coins. It was meant to be the inheritance of you and your children, but now you've lost it. You could have owned the largest pearl in existence, but evidently, it was not meant to be."

The man started wailing like a woman in childbirth. The bird [said], "Didn't

I just say, *Don't grieve for what's in the past?* And also, *Don't believe an absurdity?* My entire body doesn't weigh as much as ten copper coins. How could I have a pearl that heavy inside me?'

The man came to his senses. "All right. Tell me Number Three."

"Yes. You've made such good use of the first two!"

Don't give advice to someone who's groggy and falling asleep. Don't throw seeds on the sand. Some torn places cannot be patched.

Rumi

When Death is Not Death

A certain man was believed to have died and was being prepared for burial, when he revived.

He sat up, but he was so shocked at the scene surrounding him that he fainted.

He was put in a coffin, and the funeral party set off for the cemetery.

Just as they arrived at the grave, he regained consciousness, lifted the coffin lid, and cried out for help.

'It is not possible that he has revived,' said the mourners, 'because he has been certified dead by competent experts.'

'But I am alive!'shouted the man.

He appealed to a well-known and impartial scientist and jurisprudent who was present.

'Just a moment,' said the expert.

He then turned to the mourners, counting them. 'Now, we have heard what the alleged deceased has had to say. You fifty witnesses tell me what you regard as the truth.'

'He is dead,' said the witnesses.

'Bury him!' said the expert.

And so he was buried.

Sufi

❧❧❧❧❧❧❧

ATTACHMENTS ARE ENTANGLEMENTS

❧❧❧❧❧❧❧

The enemy is more easily overcome if he be not suffered to enter the door of our hearts, but be resisted without the gate at his first knock.

Thomas à Kempis

❧❧❧❧❧❧❧

Dropping the "I"

Disciple: I have come to offer you my service.
Master: If you dropped the "I," service would automatically follow.

❧❧❧❧❧❧❧

He who holds back rising anger like a rolling chariot, him I call a real driver; other people are but holding the reins.

Guatama Buddha

❧❧❧❧❧❧❧

Abbot Macarius said: If, wishing to correct another, you are moved to anger, you gratify your own passion. Do not lose yourself in order to save another.

Desert Fathers

❧❧❧❧❧❧❧

Speak when you are angry and you will make the best speech you will ever regret.

Ambrose Bierce

A philosopher, having made an appointment to dispute with Nasrudin, called and found him away from home.

Infuriated, he picked up a piece of chalk and wrote "Stupid Oaf" on Nasrudin's gate.

As soon as he got home and saw this, Mulla rushed to the philosopher's house.

"I had forgotten," he said, "that you were to call. And I apologize for not having been at home. Of course, I remembered the appointment as soon as I saw that you had left your name on my door."

Sufi

I have learned through bitter experience the one supreme lesson to conserve my anger, and as heat conserved is transmuted into energy, even so our anger controlled can be transmuted into a power that can move the world.

Mahatma Gandhi

I was thinking, not without bitterness, why all the most disagreeable people are attracted here, and why on earth will they always sit near me, or be shown to sit next to me? Why must I suffer such additional difficulties when the physical conditions are already difficult enough and hard to bear. And suddenly the cognition came: he is training me to detach my mind at will from all that which I do not wish to notice. To conquer the small irritations. Immediately the full significance of it became clear; here is partly the answer to the fact that he can live with his family without ever being disturbed. He does not need to go into samadhi to escape the physical conditions; and he is teaching me to do the same.

Irina Tweedie

Freedom from desire
Leads to inward peace.

Lao-Tse

❦❦❦❦❦❦❦

Two monks journeying home came to the banks of a fast-flowing river, where they met a young woman unable to cross the current alone. One of the monks picked her up in his arms and set her safely on her feet on the other side and the two monks continued on their travels. The monk who had crossed the river alone could finally restrain himself no longer and began to rebuke his brother, "Do you not know it is against our rules to touch a young woman? You have broken the holy vows."

The other monk answered, "Brother, I left that young woman on the banks of the river. Are you still carrying her?"

Zen

❦❦❦❦❦❦❦

Do not be dismayed, daughters, at the number of things which you have to consider before setting out on this Divine journey, which is the royal road to Heaven. By taking this road we gain such precious treasures that it is no wonder if the cost seems to us a high one. The time will come when we shall realize that all we have paid has been nothing at all by comparison with the greatness of our prize.

Saint Teresa of Ávila

❦❦❦❦❦❦❦

Man Believes What He Thinks is True

Teaching, as was his custom, during the ordinary business of life, Sheikh Abu Tahir Harami rode his donkey one day into a market-place, a disciple following behind.

At the sight of him, a man called out: 'Look, here comes the ancient unbeliever!'

Harami's pupil, his wrath aroused, shouted at the defamer. Before long there was a fierce altercation in progress.

The Sufi calmed his disciple, saying: 'If you will only cease this tumult, I will show you how you can escape this kind of trouble.'

They went together to the old man's house. The sheikh told his follower to bring him a box of letters. 'Look at these. They are all letters addressed to me. But they are couched in different terms. Here someone calls me "Sheikh of Islam"; there, "Sublime Teacher." Another says I am the "Wise One of the Twin Sanctuaries." And there are others.

'Observe how each styles me in accordance with what he considers me to be. But I am none of these things. Each man calls another just what he thinks him to be. This is what the unfortunate one in the market-place has just done. And yet you take exception to it. Why do you do so—since it is the general rule of life?'

Sufi

Do not let your peace depend on the hearts of men; whatever they say about you, good or bad, you are not because of it another man, for as you are, you are.

Thomas à Kempis

Mulla Nasrudin was walking along an alleyway one day when a man fell from a roof and landed on top of him. The other man was unhurt—but the Mulla was taken to the hospital.

"What teaching do you infer from this event, Master?" one of his disciples asked him.

"Avoid belief in inevitability, even if cause and effect seem inevitable! Shun theoretical questions like: 'If a man falls off a roof, will his neck be broken?' *He* fell—but *my* neck is broken!"

Sufi

My mind withdrew its thoughts from experience, extracting itself from the contradictory throng of sensuous images, that it might find out what that light was wherein it was bathed . . . . And thus, with the flash of one hurried glance, it attained to the vision of That Which Is.

Saint Augustine

The Truth Shop

I could hardly believe my eyes when I saw the name of the shop:
THE TRUTH SHOP.

The saleswoman was very polite: What type of truth did I wish to purchase, partial or whole? The whole truth, of course. No deceptions for me, no defenses, no rationalizations. I wanted my truth plain and unadulterated. She waved me on to another side of the store.

The salesman there pointed to the price tag. "The price is very high, sir," he said. "What is it?" I asked, determined to get the whole truth, no matter what it cost. "Your security, sir," he answered.

I came away with a heavy heart. I still need the safety of my unquestioned beliefs.

The Devil and his Friend

The devil once went for a walk with a friend. They saw a man ahead of them stoop down and pick up something from the ground.

"What did that man find?" asked the friend.

"A piece of truth," said the devil.

"Doesn't that disturb you?" asked the friend.

"No," said the devil, "I shall let him make a belief out of it."

There is a story that Moses was passing through a country with Khidr, who was his murshid when Moses was being prepared for prophethood. Moses was first given the lesson of discipline, to keep quiet under all circumstances. When they were walking through the beauty of nature, the teacher and pupil both were quiet. The teacher was exalted in seeing the beauty of nature; the pupil also felt it.

And so they arrived at the bank of a river, where Moses saw a little child drowning and the mother crying aloud, for she could not help. Then Moses could not keep his lips closed; he had to break his discipline and say, "Master, save him, the child is drowning!" The murshid said, "Quiet!" Moses could not keep quiet. He said again, "Master, Master, save him! The child is drowning!" Khidr said, "Quiet!" and Moses was quiet.

But the mind of Moses was restless; he did not know what to think. "Can the master be so thoughtless, so inconsiderate, so cruel, or is the master powerless?" he asked himself. He could not understand which was which; he did not dare to think such a thought, and yet it made him very uncomfortable.

As they went further they saw a boat sinking, and Moses said, "Master, that boat is sinking, it is going down." The master again ordered him to be quiet; so then Moses was quiet, but he was still most uncomfortable.

When they arrived home, he said, "Master, I would have thought that you would save that little innocent child from drowning, and that you would save that boat which was going down in the water. But you did nothing. I cannot understand; I would like to have an explanation." The master said, "What you saw I saw also. We both saw, so there was no use in your telling me, for I knew.

If I had thought that it was better to interfere, I could have done it. Why did you take the trouble to tell me, and spoil your vow of silence?" He continued, "The child who was drowning was going to bring about a conflict between two nations, and thousands and thousands of lives were going to be destroyed in that conflict. When he was drowned this averted the other danger which was to come." Moses looked at him with great surprise. Then Khidr said, "The boat that was sinking was a boat of pirates, and was sailing to wreck a large ship full of pilgrims and then take what was left in the ship and bring it home. Do you think that you and I can be judge of things? The Judge is behind it. He knows His actions; He knows His work. When you were told to be quiet, it was to keep your lips closed and to observe everything silently, as I was doing."

There is a Persian verse which says, "It is the gardener who knows which plant to rear and which to cut down."

Sufi, retold by Hazrat Inayat Khan

On my pilgrimage a lot of cars stopped and people invited me to ride. Some thought walking meant hitchhiking. I told them I did not cheat God— you don't cheat about counting miles on a pilgrimage.

I remember one day as I walked along the highway a very nice car stopped and the man inside said to me, "How wonderful that you are following your calling!" I replied, " I certainly think that everyone should be doing what he or she feels is the right thing to do."

He then began telling me what he felt motivated toward, and it was a good thing that needed doing. I got quite enthusiastic about it and took it for granted that he was doing it. I said, "That's wonderful! How are you getting along with it?" And he answered, "Oh, I'm not doing it. That kind of work doesn't *pay* anything."

I shall never forget how desperately unhappy that man was. In this materialistic age we have such a false criteria by which to measure success. We measure it in terms of dollars, in terms of material things. But happiness and inner peace do not lie in that direction. If you know but do not do, you are a very unhappy person indeed.

Peace Pilgrim

'What think you Subhuti? Suppose a disciple has attained the degree of *arahat* (full enlightenment), could he entertain within his mind any such arbitrary conception as "I have become a fully enlightened one?"'

'No, honoured of the worlds! Because speaking truly, there is no such thing as a fully enlightened one. Should a disciple who has attained such a degree of enlightenment cherish within his mind such an arbitrary conception as "I have become an *arahat*," he would soon be grasping after such things as his own selfhood, other selves, living beings and a universal self.'

Diamond Sutra

ೞಎೞಎೞಎೞಎ

If thou shouldst say, "It is enough, I have reached perfection," all is lost. For it is the function of perfection to make one know one's imperfection.

Saint Augustine

ೞಎೞಎೞಎೞಎ

The soul's impurity consists in bad judgments, and purification consists in producing in it right judgments, and the pure soul is one which has right judgments.

Epictetus

ೞಎೞಎೞಎೞಎ

"There are two roads: the road of dhyana, the slow one; and the road of tyaga, of complete renunciation, of surrender. This is the direct road, the path of fire, the path of love."

"But will you not treat a woman differently from a man? A woman is more tender; the psychology of a woman and of a man is different!"

He shook his head. "The training is somewhat different. But it does not mean that because you are a woman you will get preferential treatment."

"But don't you see I am at odds against your Indian disciples?" I exclaimed. And he shook his head. "No, it is always difficult. For everybody. If it is not one thing, then it is another. Human beings are covered with so much conditioning."

Irina Tweedie

ೞಎೞಎೞಎೞಎ

A tale is told of a young Buddhist monk who worried a lot. While walking through the forest to return to his monastery he came upon an old Zen master. Delighted to have found an audience for his obsessions, he tried to strike up a conversation with this seemingly carefree older man.

The young monk talked a great deal, mostly about himself. The old man listened and smiled, but did not seem to have much to say. In the midst of his monologue, the young man declared, "I became a monk to attain spiritual enlightenment. For a long while I was afraid I would never attain a saintly attitude, but my years of spiritual sacrifice have paid off and now I have become quite humble."

"How about you?" he asked the old man, "Are you humble?"

After a few moments of quiet concentration, the master replied, "I don't really know. I've never thought much about it."

The world became a very interesting place to live. I came to know the thoughts of people, the reasons why they came to Guruji. I used to tell one of his disciples who sat near me: this one comes because his child is ill; this other one because he has a court case and wants some help and advice; that man on the right is ill and hopes that Guruji will heal him, and so on . . . . Of course I was delighted. Bhai Sahib did not take any notice of me, was talking to others, and I sat there full of wonder and delight, observing everything around me.

Then, one day, when he turned to me and said something, I took the opportunity and told him how pleased I was that only after such a short time with him I was progressing so fast.

"*Oh?*" he lifted his eyebrows, "*and why so?*" I told him, describing in detail what I saw and telling him that I knew the reason why each one came to him.

He listened. His expression was that of slight irony; then he gave me a sideways look and turned away to speak to others.

The ability to know the thoughts of people vanished, however, and after three days of waiting for it to return, she stormed:

"You took it away from me!"

"*Of course!*" he answered quickly. "*Just look at you! You were blown up like a balloon! Are you after Absolute Truth or are you after illusions? How will the self go if you continue like this?*"

Irina Tweedie

REAL OR ILLUSION

Holiness in the Present Moment

The Japanese warrior was captured by his enemies and thrown into prison.

At night he could not sleep for he was convinced that he would be tortured the next morning.

Then the words of his master came to his mind. "Tomorrow is not real. The only reality is now."

So he came to the present—and fell asleep.

What Am I Leaving Out?

I knew there were many interesting sights, but I didn't want any more of the LITTLE answers. I wanted the big answer. So I asked the guestmaster to show me to the House of the Christian God.

I sat myself down, quite willing to wait for the big answer. I remained silent all day, far into the night. I looked Him in the eye. I guess He was looking me in the eye. Late, late at night I seemed to hear a voice, "What are you leaving out?" I looked around. I heard it again, "What are you leaving out?" Was it my imagination? Soon it was all around me, whispering, roaring, "What are you leaving out? WHAT ARE YOU LEAVING OUT?"

Was I cracking up? I managed to get to my feet and head for the door. I guess I wanted the comfort of a human face or a human voice. Nearby was the corridor where some of the monks live. I knocked on one cell.

"What do you want?" came a sleepy voice.

"What am I leaving out?"

"Me," he answered.

I went to the next door.

"What do you want?"

"What am I leaving out?"

"Me."

A third cell, a fourth, all the same.

I thought to myself, "They're all stuck on themselves." I left the building in disgust. Just then the sun was coming up. I had never spoken to the sun before, but I heard myself pleading, "What am I leaving out?"

The sun too answered, "Me." That finished me.

I threw myself flat on the ground. Then the earth said, "ME."

Father Theophane

The Egg

Nasrudin earned his living selling eggs. Someone came to his shop one day and said, "Guess what I have in my hand."

"Give me a clue," said Nasrudin.

"I shall give you several: It has the shape of an egg, the size of an egg. It looks like an egg, tastes like an egg, and smells like an egg. Inside it is yellow and white. It is liquid before it is cooked, becomes thick when heated. It was, moreover, laid by a hen."

"Aha! I know!" said Nasrudin. "It is some sort of cake!"

Sufi

The Formula

The mystic was back from the desert. "Tell us," they said, "what God is like."

But how could he ever tell them what he had experienced in his heart? Can God be put into words?

He finally gave them a formula—so inaccurate, so inadequate—in the hope that some of them might be tempted to experience it for themselves.

They seized upon the formula. They made it a sacred text. They imposed it on others as a holy belief. They went to great pains to spread it in foreign lands. Some even gave their lives for it.

The mystic was sad. It might have been better if he had said nothing.

He who binds to himself a joy
Doth the winged life destroy.
But he who kisses the joy as it flies
Lives in Eternity's sunrise.

William Blake

Chapter II

Training the Heart and Mind

"Mulla, Mulla, my son has written from the Abode of Learning to say that he has completely finished his studies!"

"Console yourself, madam, with the thought that God will no doubt send him more."

Sufi

🐦🐦🐦🐦🐦

Nobody grows old merely by living a number of years; people grow old by deserting their ideals. Years wrinkle the skin, but giving up enthusiasm wrinkles the soul.

Zoroaster

🐦🐦🐦🐦🐦

Once he met a Zen novice who had just finished his first year of living in a monastery. [Thomas] Merton asked the novice what he had learned during the course of his novitiate, half expecting to hear of encounters with enlightenment, discoveries of the spirit, perhaps even altered states of consciousness. But the novice replied that during his first year in the contemplative life he had simply learned to open and close doors.

99

"Learned to open and close doors." The quiet discipline of not acting impetuously, of not running around slamming doors, of not hurrying from one place to another was where this novice had to begin (and perhaps end) in the process of spiritual growth. *"Learned to open and close doors."* Merton loved the answer and often retold the story, for it exemplified for him "play" at its very best—doing the ordinary, while being absorbed in it intensely and utterly.

I would like to mention some preparations that were required of me. The first preparation is to take *a right attitude toward life.* This means, stop being an escapist! Stop being a surface liver who stays right in the froth of the surface. There are millions of these people, and they never find anything really worthwhile. Be willing to face life squarely and get down beneath the surface of life where the verities and realities are to be found. That's what we are doing here now.

There's the whole matter of having a meaningful attitude toward the problems that life may set before you. If only you could see the whole picture, if you knew the whole story, you would realize that no problem ever comes to you that does not have a purpose in your life, that cannot contribute to your inner growth.

Peace Pilgrim

The Poet and the Physician

A poet went to see a doctor. He said to him: 'I have all kinds of terrible symptoms. I am unhappy and uncomfortable, my hair and my arms and legs are as if tortured.'

The doctor answered: 'Is it not true that you have not yet given out your latest poetic composition?'

'That is true,' said the poet.

'Very well,' said the physician, 'be good enough to recite.'

He did so, and, at the doctor's orders, said his lines again and again. Then the doctor said: 'Stand up, for you are now cured. What you had inside had affected your outside. Now that it is released, you are well again.'

Sufi

If thou canst walk on water
Thou art no better than a straw.
If thou canst fly in the air
Thou art no better than a fly.
Conquer thy heart
That thou mayest become somebody.

Ansari

He who is not tempted, what does he know? And he who is not tried, what are the things he knows?

Have patience with all things, but chiefly have patience with yourself. Do not lose courage in considering your own imperfections, but instantly set about remedying them—every day begin the task anew.

Saint Francis de Sales

He who is not tempted, what does he know? And he who is not tried, what are the things he knows?

Ecclesiasticus

Dandelions

A man who took great pride in his lawn found himself with a large crop of dandelions. He tried every method he knew to get rid of them. Still they plagued him.

Finally he wrote the Department of Agriculture. He enumerated all the things he had tried and closed his letter with the question: "What shall I do now?"

In due course the reply came: "We suggest you learn to love them."

Loving Kindness

May every creature abound in well-being and peace.
May every living being, weak or strong, the long and the small
The short and the medium-sized, the mean and the great
May every living being, seen or unseen, those dwelling far off,

Those near by, those already born, those waiting to be born
May all attain inward peace
Let no one deceive another
Let no one despise another in any situation
Let no one, from antipathy or hatred, wish evil to anyone at all.
Just as a mother, with her own life, protects her only son from hurt
So within yourself foster a limitless concern for every living creature.
Display a heart of boundless love for all the world
In all its height and depth and broad extent
Love unrestrained, without hate or enmity.
Then as you stand or walk, sit or lie, until overcome by drowsiness
Devote your mind entirely to this, it is known as living here life divine.

Buddhist Prayer

The Five Hundred Gold Pieces

One of Junaid's followers came to him with a purse containing five hundred gold pieces.
'Have you any more money than this?' asked the Sufi.
'Yes, I have.'
'Do you desire more?'
'Yes, I do.'
'Then you must keep it, for you are more in need than I; for I have nothing and desire nothing. You have a great deal and still want more.'

Sufi

We ought to fly away from earth to heaven as quickly as we can; and to fly away is to become like God, as far as this is possible; and to become like him, is to become holy, just, and wise.

Plato

Instead of becoming discouraged, I said to myself: God cannot inspire unrealizable desires. I can, then, in spite of my littleness, aspire to holiness. It is impossible for me to grow up, and so I must bear with myself such as I am with all my imperfections. But I want to seek out a means of going to heaven by a little way, a way that is very straight, very short, and totally new.

Saint Thérèse of Lisieux, *The Story of a Soul*

The Lion and the Mouse

One day a great lion lay asleep in the sunshine. A little mouse ran across his paw and wakened him. The great lion was just going to eat him up when the little mouse cried, "Oh, please, let me go, sir. Some day I may help you."

The lion laughed at the thought that the little mouse could be of any use to him. But he was a good-natured lion, and he set the mouse free.

Not long after, the lion was caught in a net. He tugged and pulled with all his might, but the ropes were too strong. Then he roared loudly. The little mouse heard him, and ran to the spot.

"Be still, dear Lion, and I will set you free. I will gnaw the ropes."

With his sharp little teeth, the mouse cut the ropes, and the lion came out of the net.

"You laughed at me once," said the mouse. "You thought I was too little to do you a good turn. But see, you owe your life to a poor little mouse."

Aesop

Abide in peace, banish cares, take no account of all that happens, and you will serve God according to His good pleasure, and rest in Him.

Saint John of the Cross

The spiritual life is the real life; all else is illusion and deception. Only those who are attached to God alone are truly free. Only those who live up to the highest light live in harmony. All who act upon their highest motivations become a power for good. It is not important that others be noticeably affected: results should never be sought or desired. Know that every right thing you do—every good word you say—every positive thought you think—has good effect.

Peace Pilgrim

In every Nation there are wise and good men. These should be appointed Chiefs. They should be the advisers of their people and work for the good of all people, and all their power comes from the "Great Peace." A chief must never forget the Creator of mankind, never forget to ask Him for help. The Creator will guide our thoughts and strengthen us as we work to be faithful to our sacred trust and restore harmony among all peoples, all living creatures, and Mother Earth . . . . We were instructed to carry a love for one another and to show a great respect for all the beings of this earth . . . . In our ways, spiritual consciousness is the highest form of politics . . . . When people cease to respect and express gratitude for these many things, then all life will be destroyed, and human life on this planet will come to an end.

These are our times and our responsibilities. Every human being has a sacred duty to protect the welfare of our Mother Earth, from whom all life comes. In order to do this we must recognize the enemy—the one within us. We must begin with ourselves . . . .

We must live in harmony with the Natural World and recognize that excessive exploitation can only lead to our own destruction. We cannot trade the welfare of our future generations for profit now. We must abide by the Natural Law or be victim of its ultimate reality.

Leon Shenandoah/Native American Elder
Six Nations Iroquois Confederacy

True happiness comes from a sense of inner peace and contentment, which in turn must be achieved through cultivation of altruism, of love, of compassion, and through the elimination of anger, selfishness, and greed.

Tenzin Gyatso, the 14th Dalai Lama of Tibet

Out of compassion I destroy the darkness of their ignorance. From within them I light the lamp of wisdom and dispel all darkness from their lives.

Sri Krishna, *Bhagavad Gita*

Prayer and Meditation

The Temple Bells

The temple was built on an island and it held a thousand bells. Bells big and small, fashioned by the finest craftsmen in the world. When the wind blew or a storm raged, all the bells would peal out in a symphony that would send the heart of the hearer into raptures.

But over the centuries the island sank into the sea and, with it, the temple bells. An ancient legend said that the bells continued to peal out, ceaselessly, and could be heard by anyone who would listen. Inspired by this legend, a young man traveled thousands of miles, determined to hear those bells. He sat for days on the shore, facing the vanished island, and listened with all his might. But all he could hear was the sound of the sea. He made every effort to block it out. But to no avail; the sound of the sea seemed to flood the world.

He kept at his task for weeks. Each time he got disheartened he would listen to the village pundits, who spoke with unction of the mysterious legend.

Then his heart would be aflame . . . only to become discouraged again when weeks of further effort yielded no results.

Finally, he decided to give up the attempt. Perhaps he was not destined to hear the bells. Perhaps the legend was not true. It was his final day, and he went to the shore to say goodbye to the sea and the sky and the wind and the coconut trees. He lay on the sand, and for the first time, listened to the sound of the sea. Soon he was so lost in the sound that he was barely conscious of himself, so deep was the silence that the sound produced.

In the depth of that silence, he heard it! The tinkle of a tiny bell followed by another, and another and another . . . and soon every one of the thousand temple bells was pealing out in harmony, and his heart was rapt in joyous ecstasy.

That prayer has great power which a person makes with all his might. It makes a sour heart sweet, a sad heart merry, a poor heart rich, a foolish heart wise, a timid heart brave, a sick heart well, a blind heart full of sight, a cold heart ardent. It draws down the great God into the little heart, it drives the hungry soul up into the fullness of God, it brings together two lovers, God and the soul in a wondrous place where they speak much of love.

Mechthild of Magdeburg

White Man Gets Everything Wrong

"He says we're warlike when we're peaceful. He calls us savages, but he's the savage. See, he calls this headdress a warbonnet. Sure, we used it in war, but most of the time it was for ceremony, not war. Each feather stands for a good deed and I have thirty-six in mine. It's not about war; it's about who we are. When we sing songs he calls them war songs. But they're not war songs, they're prayers to God. We have drums, so White Man calls them war drums; but they're not for war, they're for talking to God. There's no such thing as a war drum. He sees how our warriors paint their faces, so he calls it war paint. But it's not for war, it's to make it so God can see our faces clearly if we have to die. So how can we talk to the White Man of peace when he only knows war?"

Mathew King, Lakota

When Brother Bruno was at prayer one night he was disturbed by the croaking of a bullfrog. All his attempts to disregard the sound were unsuccessful, so he shouted from his window, "Quiet! I'm at my prayers."

Now Brother Bruno was a saint, so his command was instantly obeyed. Every living creature held its voice so as to create a silence that would be favorable to prayer.

But now another sound intruded on Bruno's worship—an inner voice that said, "Maybe God is as pleased with the croaking of that frog as with the chanting of your psalms." "What can please the ears of God in the croak of a frog?" was Bruno's scornful rejoinder. But the voice refused to give up. "Why would you think God invented the sound?"

Bruno decided to find out why. He leaned out of his window and gave the order, "Sing!" The bullfrog's measured croaking filled the air to the ludicrous accompaniment of all the frogs in the vicinity. And as Bruno attended to the sound, their voices ceased to jar for he discovered that, if he stopped resisting them, they actually enriched the silence of the night.

With that discovery Bruno's heart became harmonious with the universe and, for the first time in his life, he understood what it means to pray.

But they for whom I am the supreme goal, who do all work renouncing self for me and meditate on me with single-hearted devotion, these I will swiftly rescue from death's vast sea, for their consciousness has entered into me.

Sri Krishna, *Bhagavad Gita*

Meditation brings wisdom; lack of meditation leaves ignorance. Know well what leads you forward and what holds you back, and choose the path that leads to wisdom.

Guatama Buddha

Those who eat too much or eat too little, who sleep too much or sleep too little, will not succeed in meditation. But those who are temperate in eating and sleeping, work and recreation, will come to the end of sorrow through meditation.

Sri Krishna, *Bhagavad Gita*

Even as a tortoise draws in its limbs, the wise can draw in their senses at will.

Sri Krishna, *Bhagavad Gita*

Another brother asked the same elder, Abbot Theodore, and began to question him and to inquire about things which he had never yet put into practice himself. The elder said to him: As yet you have not found a ship, and you have not put your baggage aboard, and you have not started to cross the sea: can you talk as if you had already arrived in that city to which you planned to go? When you have put into practice the thing you are talking about, then speak from knowledge of the thing itself!

Desert Fathers

Like the gates of a city, we have to open the organs of sense-perception in order to satisfy essential needs; but, in so doing, we must take care not to give access at the same time to warlike tribes that seek to attack us.

Philokalia 3:63

All this talk and turmoil and noise and movement and desire is outside of the veil; within the veil is silence and calm and rest.

Bayazid Al-Bistami

But, you see, you are not educated to be alone. Do you ever go out for a walk by yourself? It is very important to go out alone, to sit under a tree—not with a book, not with a companion, but by yourself—and observe the falling of a leaf, hear the lapping of the water, the fisherman's song, watch the flight of a bird, and of your own thoughts as they chase each other across the space of your mind. If you are able to be alone and watch these things, then you will discover extraordinary riches which no government can tax, no human agency can corrupt, and which can never be destroyed.

J. Krishnamurti, *Think on These Things*

As a fish hooked and left on the sand thrashes about in agony, the mind being trained in meditation trembles all over, desperate to escape the hand of Mara.

Dhammapada

Hsin-Hsin Ming

The wise person does not strive;
The ignorant man ties himself up . . .
If you work on your mind with your mind,
How can you avoid an immense confusion?

Seng-ts'an

It is not to be learned by world-flight, running away from things, turning solitary and going apart from the world. Rather, one must learn an inner solitude, wherever or with whomsoever he may be.

Meister Eckhart: A Modern Translation

ê♦ê♦ê♦ê♦ê♦ê♦

The Indian sage, Narada, was a devotee of the Lord Hari. So great was his devotion that he was one day tempted to think that in all the world there was no one who loved God more than he.

The Lord read his heart and said, "Narada, go to this town on the banks of the Ganges, for a devotee of mine dwells there. Living in his company will do you good."

Narada went and found a farmer who rose early in the morning, pronounced the name of Hari only once, then lifted his plough and went out to his fields where he worked all day. Just before he fell asleep at night, he pronounced the name of Hari once again. Narada thought, "How can this rustic be a devotee of God? I see him immersed all day in his worldly occupations."

Then the Lord said to Narada, "Fill a bowl to the brim with milk and walk all around the city. Then come back without spilling a single drop." Narada did as he was told.

"How many times did you remember me in the course of your walk around the city?" asked the Lord.

"Not once, Lord," said Narada. "How could I when you commanded me to watch that bowl of milk?"

The Lord said, "That bowl so absorbed your attention that you forgot me altogether. But look at that peasant who, though burdened with the cares of supporting a family, remembers me twice every day!"

ê♦ê♦ê♦ê♦ê♦ê♦

Prayer to the Great Spirit

O great spirit
Whose voice I hear in the wind
Whose breath gives life to the world
Hear me
I come to ask you as one of your many children
I am small and weak
I need your strength and wisdom
May I walk in beauty
Make my eyes behold the red-and-purple sunset
Make my hands respect the things that you have made
    and my ears sharp to hear your voice
Make me wise so that I may know
      the things that you have taught your children
      the lessons that you have hidden in every leaf and rock
Make me strong
Not to be superior to my brothers
But to be able to fight my greatest enemy—myself
Make me ever ready to come to you with straight eyes

So that when life fades as the faded sunset
My spirit will come to you without shame

Traditional Native American

❦❦❦❦❦❦❦

Draw near to God, not by rites and ceremonies, but by inward disposition. Heaven is neither a place nor a time.

Florence Nightingale

❦❦❦❦❦❦❦

Health is the best gift, contentment the best wealth, trust the best kinsman, nirvana the greatest joy. Drink the nectar of the dharma in the depths of meditation, and become free from fear and sin.

Dhammapada

❦❦❦❦❦❦❦

A monk was walking in the monastery grounds one day when he heard a bird sing.

He listened, spellbound. It seemed to him that never before had he heard, really heard, the song of a bird.

When the singing stopped, he returned to the monastery and discovered, to his dismay, that he was a stranger to his fellow monks, and they to him.

It was only gradually that they and he discovered that he was returning after centuries. Because his listening was total, time had stopped and he had slipped into eternity.

Christian

❦❦❦❦❦❦❦

A cobbler came to Rabbi Isaac of Ger and said, "Tell me what to do about my morning prayer. My customers are poor men who have only one pair of shoes. I pick up their shoes late in the evening and work on them most of the night; at dawn there is still work to be done if the men are to have their shoes ready before they go to work. Now my question is: What should I do about my morning prayer?"

"What have you been doing till now?" the Rabbi asked.

"Sometimes I rush through the prayer quickly and get back to my work— but then I feel bad about it. At other times I let the hour of prayer go by. Then too I feel a sense of loss and every now and then, as I raise my hammer from the shoes, I can almost hear my heart sigh, 'What an unlucky man I am, that I am not able to make my morning prayer.'"

Said the Rabbi, "If I were God I would value that sigh more than the prayer."

Jewish Folktale

&ℯℯℯℯℯℯℯℯ

Learn self-conquest, persevere thus for a time, and you will perceive very clearly the advantage which you gain from it. As soon as you apply yourself to orison, you will at once feel your senses gather themselves together: they seem like bees which return to the hive and there shut themselves up to work at the making of honey . . . . God thus rewards the violence which your soul has been doing to itself . . . . At the first call of the will, they (the senses) come back more and more quickly. At last, after countless exercises of this kind, God disposes them to a state of utter rest and of perfect contemplation.

Saint Teresa of Ávila

He who interrupts the course of his spiritual exercises and prayer is like a man who allows a bird to escape from his hand; he can hardly catch it again.

Saint John of the Cross

It is less hard to check the downward flow of a river than for one who prays to check the turbulence of the intellect when he wishes, preventing it from fragmenting itself among visible things and concentrating it on the higher realities kindred to it. This is so in spite of the fact that to check the flow of a river is contrary to nature, while to check the turbulence of the intellect accords with nature.

Philokalia 3:61

He who has dedicated his life to this kind of service will find before long that others come to him—perhaps a few at first, but later many more—to pile on his sturdy shoulders the burdens and sufferings, the perplexities and gropings which they find so difficult to deal with themselves.

Paul Brunton

᠂᠄᠊᠄᠊᠄᠊᠄᠊᠄᠊

Let me tell you a story about an answer to prayer. I was picked up late one night by a young policeman as I was walking along a lonely highway. I believe he was thinking in terms of protective custody. He said to me, "Why, nobody in this town would walk out along this highway at this time of night."

I said to him, "Well, you see, I walk completely without fear. Therefore I'm not attracting things which are not good. It says, *That which I feared came upon me.* But I fear nothing and expect only good."

He took me in anyhow, and I found myself in a cell. The floor was littered with old newspapers and cigarette butts and every old thing. The accommodations consisted of a single mattress on the floor and four ragged blankets. There were two women attempting to sleep together on that single mattress. They told me there had been eight women in that cell the night before with those accommodations. There was a rather nice feeling among the prisoners in general. They said to me, "You'll need to have two blankets because you'll be sleeping on the floor." So I took a newspaper and cleared a place on the floor, then put one blanket down and the other blanket over me and slept comfortably enough.

It wasn't the first time I had slept on a cement floor, nor the last. If you're relaxed you can sleep anywhere. When I woke up in the morning I saw this man staring through the bars. I said to him, "What time does court convene?" He said, "I don't know." I said, "Well, aren't you a policeman?" "No," he said, "I just like to look at the girls." It was one of the town sports. Anyone could come in right off the street and see what they had there today: "Let's go look at the girls!"

One of the women was middle aged and was being held for being drunk and disorderly. It was her seventh offense, she told me, so it wasn't so hard on her. But the other was an eighteen year old girl. She felt her entire life was ruined because of this experience. I said, "It's my second time and I certainly don't think my life is ruined!" I got her all cheered up and we talked about what she'd do when she got out. She was to get out that day or the next day.

Then they changed the guards. I never saw a matron. The new guard saw me and said, "What are you doing in there? I saw your picture in the newspaper. I heard you over the air." Then they just let me go.

But before I left I got a broom from the man who cleaned up around there and gave it to the girls so they could clean up their cell. I also got them a comb; their hair was all matted. They had been there about a week without a comb.

What I really wanted to tell you is that the eighteen year old girl was a deeply religious person. She had been desperately praying for help. I believe that I was picked up off the highway that night and set behind prison bars in answer to her prayers.

Peace Pilgrim

A century ago, a young student at the great Oxford University in England was taking an important examination in religious studies. The examination question for this day was to write about the religious and spiritual meaning in the miracle of Christ turning water into wine. For two hours he sat in the crowded classroom while other students filled their pages with long essays, to show their understanding. The exam time was almost over and this one student had not written a single word. The proctor came over to him and insisted that he commit something to the paper before turning it in. The young Lord Byron simply picked up his hand and penned the following line: "The water met its Master, and blushed."

Christian

Once the Master was at prayer. The disciples came up to him and said, "Sir, teach us how to pray." This is how he taught them . . .

Two men were once walking through a field when they saw an angry bull. Instantly, they made for the nearest fence with the bull in hot pursuit. It soon became evident to them that they were not going to make it, so one man shouted to the other, "We've had it! Nothing can save us. Say a prayer. Quick!"

The other shouted back, "I've never prayed in my life and I don't have a prayer for this occasion."

"Never mind. The bull is catching up with us. Any prayer will do."

"Well, I'll say the one I remember my father used to say before meals: For what we are about to receive, Lord, make us truly grateful."

Christian

After this manner therefore pray ye: Our Father which art in heaven, Hallowed be thy name.

Thy kingdom come. Thy will be done in earth, as *it is* in heaven.

Give us this day our daily bread.

And forgive us our debts, as we forgive our debtors.

And lead us not into temptation, but deliver us from evil: For thine is the kingdom, and the power, and the glory, for ever. Amen.

The Gospel According to Saint Matthew

If a person withdraws into himself, with all his powers, mental and physical (i.e., agents of his soul), he comes at last to a condition in which he has no ideas and no limitations and in which he exists without activity of inner or outward life.

He should observe, then, whether or not he is moved to come back to life, but if he finds that he has no urge to get back to work or responsible activity, then he should break loose and get to work of some kind, mental or physical. For a man should never be content with such indulgence however good it may be or seem to be, which really does violence to his nature and of which it could be said that he is doing no work, but is merely worked upon, for we must learn to co-operate with God.

Not that one should give up, neglect or forget his inner life for a moment, but he must learn to work in it, with it and out of it, so that the unity of his soul may break out into his activities and his activities shall lead him back to that unity. In this way one is taught to work as a free man should [dispassionately]. Keep your eye on the functioning of your inner life and start from there—to read, or pray, or to do any needed outward deed. If, however, the outward life interferes with the inner, then follow the inner; but if the two can go on together, that is best of all and then man is working together with God.

Meister Eckhart, *The Talks of Instruction*

No Distance

I asked each of the monks I met this question: "What great blunder have you made?"

One answered, "There was a stone in my room, and I did not love it."

Another said, "They called me a Christian, but I did not become Christ."

I asked the first, "What do you mean? I don't understand. You didn't love that stone . . . ."

"I just didn't love it. I was so close to redeeming the whole world, but I looked down on that stone."

I asked the second, "You did not become Christ? Is one supposed to become Christ?"

"I kept putting distance between myself and him—by seeking, by praying, by reading. I kept deploring the distance, but I never realized that I was creating it."

"But," I insisted, "Is one supposed to become Christ?"

His answer: "No distance."

Father Theophane

Quiet minds cannot be perplexed or frightened, but go on in fortune or misfortune at their own private pace, like a clock during a thunderstorm.

Robert Louis Stevenson

Bees surround their queen among fresh meadow-flowers; and the soul that is unceasingly in a state of compunction is surrounded and assisted by the angelic powers, for it is kindred to them.

Philokalia 3:61

Through the practice of the virtues, the outward aspects of the soul become like the silver-coated wings of a dove. Through contemplation its inward and intelligible aspects become golden. But the soul that has not in this way regained its beauty cannot soar aloft and come to rest in the abode of the blessed.

Philokalia 3:51

Those who are more adapted to the active life can prepare themselves for contemplation in the practice of the active life, while those who are more adapted to the contemplative life can take upon themselves the works of the active life so as to become yet more apt for contemplation.

Saint Thomas Aquinas

The quality of the grain is usually evident in the ear of corn; similarly, the purity of contemplation is usually evident in prayer. The grain is surrounded by a spear-like sheath in order to prevent the birds from eating it; contemplation is armed with spiritual thoughts through which to destroy the temptations that attack it.

Philokalia 3:51

The Great Silence

"Would you teach me silence?" I asked.

"Ah!"

He seemed to be pleased. "Is it the Great Silence that you want?"

"Yes, the Great Silence."

"Well, where do you think it's to be found?" he asked.

"Deep within me, I suppose. If only I could go deep within, I'm sure I'd escape the noise at last. But it's hard. Will you help me?" I knew he would. I could feel his concern, and his spirit was so silent.

"Well, I've been there," he answered. "I spent years going in. I did taste the silence there. But one day Jesus came—maybe it was my imagination—and said to me simply, 'Come, follow me.' I went out, and I've never gone back."

I was stunned. "But the silence . . ."

"I've found the Great Silence, and I've come to see that the noise was inside."

Father Theophane

LOVE

Love all that has been created by God, both the whole and every grain of sand. Love every leaf and every ray of light. Love the beasts and the birds, love the plants, love every separate fragment. If you love each separate fragment, you will understand the mystery of the whole resting in God.

F. M. Dostoevsky

Androcles and the Lion

In Rome there was once a poor slave whose name was Androcles. His master was a cruel man, and so unkind to him that at last Androcles ran away.

He hid himself in a wild wood for many days. But there was no food to be found, and he grew so weak and sick that he thought he would die. So one day he crept into a cave and lay down, and soon he was fast asleep.

After a while a great noise woke him up. A lion had come into the cave, and was roaring loudly. Androcles was very much afraid, for he felt sure that the beast would kill him. Soon, however, he saw that the lion was not angry, but that he limped as though his foot hurt him.

Then Androcles grew so bold that he took hold of the lion's lame paw to see what was the matter. The lion stood quite still, and rubbed his head against the man's shoulder. He seemed to say "I know that you will help me."

Androcles lifted the paw from the ground, and saw that it was a long, sharp thorn which hurt the lion so much. He took the end of the thorn in his fingers; then he gave a strong, quick pull, and out it came. The lion was full of joy. He jumped about like a dog, and licked the hands and feet of his new friend.

Androcles was not at all afraid after this. And when night came, he and the lion lay down and slept side by side.

For a long time, the lion brought food to Androcles every day, and the two became such good friends that Androcles found his new life a very happy one.

One day some soldiers who were passing through the wood found Androcles in the cave. They knew who he was, and so took him back to Rome.

It was the law at that time that every slave who ran away from his master should be made to fight a hungry lion. So a fierce lion was shut up for a while without food, and a time was set for the fight.

When the day came, thousands of people crowded to see the sport. They went to such places at that time very much as people now go to see a circus show, or a game of baseball.

The door opened, and poor Androcles was brought in. He was almost dead with fear, for the roars of the lion could already be heard. He looked up, and saw that there was no pity in the thousands of faces around him.

Then the hungry lion rushed in. With a single bound he reached the poor slave. Androcles gave a great cry, not of fear, but of gladness. It was his old friend, the lion of the cave.

The people, who had expected to see the man killed by the lion, were filled with wonder. They saw Androcles put his arms around the lion's neck; they saw the lion lie down at his feet, and lick them lovingly; they saw the great beast rub his head against the slave's face as though he wanted to be petted. They could not understand what it all meant.

After a while they asked Androcles to tell them about it. So he stood up before them, and, with his arm around the lion's neck, told how he and the beast had lived together in the cave.

"I am a man," he said, "but no man has ever befriended me. This poor lion alone has been kind to me and we love each other as brothers."

The people were not so bad that they could be cruel to the poor slave now. "Live and be free!" they cried. "Live and be free!"

Others cried, "Let the lion go free too! Give both of them their liberty!"

And so Androcles was set free, and the lion was given to him for his own. And they lived together in Rome for many years.

Retold by James Baldwin

You learn to speak by speaking, to study by studying, to run by running, to work by working; in just the same way, you learn to love by loving.

Saint Francis de Sales

Shakespeare says, "Love bears it out even to the edge of doom."

A disciple asked Rabbi Shmelke: 'We are commanded to love our neighbour as ourselves. How can I do this if my neighbour has wronged me?'

The rabbi answered: 'You must understand these words aright. Love your neighbour like something which you yourself are. For all souls are one. Each is a spark from the original soul, and this soul is wholly inherent in all souls, just as your soul is in all the members of your body. It may come to pass that your hand makes a mistake and strikes you. But would you then take a stick and chastise your hand, because it lacked understanding, and so increase your pain? It is the same if your neighbour, who is of one soul with you, wrongs you for lack of understanding. If you punish him, you only hurt yourself.'

The disciple went on asking: 'But if I see a man who is wicked before God, how can I love him?'

'Don't you know,' said Rabbi Shmelke, 'that the original soul came out of the essence of God, and that every human soul is a part of God? And will you have no mercy on him, when you see that one of his holy sparks has been lost in a maze, and is almost stifled?'

Martin Buber, *Tales of the Hassidim*

We are shaped and fashioned by what we love.

Johann Wolfgang von Goethe

Some day, after we have mastered the winds, the waves, and gravity, we will harness for God the energies of love; and then for the second time in the history of the world, man will have discovered fire.

Pierre Teilhard de Chardin

꩜꩜꩜꩜꩜

Love is God; that is the only God that I really recognize. Love equals God.

Mahatma Gandhi

꩜꩜꩜꩜꩜

The Good Samaritan

And Jesus answering said, A certain *man* went down from Jerusalem to Jericho, and fell among thieves, which stripped him of his raiment, and wounded *him*, and departed, leaving *him* half dead.

And by chance there came down a certain priest that way: and when he saw him, he passed by on the other side.

And likewise a Levite, when he was at the place, came and looked *on him*, and passed by on the other side.

But a certain Samaritan, as he journeyed, came where he was: and when he saw him, he had compassion *on him*.

And went to *him*, and bound up his wounds, pouring in oil and wine, and set him on his own beast, and brought him to an inn, and took care of him.

And on the morrow when he departed, he took out two pence, and gave *them* to the host, and said unto him, Take care of him; and whatsoever thou spendest more, when I come again, I will repay thee.

Which now of these three, thinkest thou, was neighbour unto him that fell among the thieves?

And he said, He that shewed mercy on him. Then said Jesus unto him, Go, and do thou likewise.

The Gospel According to Saint Luke

꩜꩜꩜꩜꩜

This is the way of peace: *Overcome evil with good, falsehood with truth, and hatred with love.*

It is hard for people to understand that all war is bad and self-defeating. People in their immaturity attempt to overcome evil with more evil, and that multiplies the evil. Only good can overcome evil.

My simple peace message is adequate—really just the message that the way of peace is the way of love. Love is the greatest power on earth. It conquers all things. One in harmony with God's law of love has more strength than an army, for one need not subdue an adversary; an adversary can be transformed.

Peace Pilgrim

He who desires to see the living God face to face should not seek Him in the empty firmament of his mind but in human love.

Dostoevsky

Where love rules, there is no will to power; and where power predominates, there love is lacking. The one is the shadow of the other.

Carl Gustav Jung

All Life is Equal

"Another of the Natural laws is that all life is equal. That's our philosophy. You have to respect life—all life, not just your own. The key word is 'respect.' Unless you respect the earth, you destroy it. Unless you respect all life as much as your own life, you become a destroyer, a murderer.

Man sometimes thinks he's been elevated to be the controller, the ruler. But he's not. He's only a part of the whole. Man's job is not to exploit but to oversee, to be a steward. Man has responsibility, not power."

Oren Lyons, Native American Elder/Onondaga

Though I speak with the tongues of men and of angels, and have not charity, I am become *as* sounding brass, or a tinkling cymbal.

And though I have *the gift of* prophecy, and understand all mysteries, and all knowledge; and though I have all faith, so that I could remove mountains, and have not charity, I am nothing.

And though I bestow all my goods to feed *the poor*, and though I give my body to be burned, and have not charity, it profiteth me nothing.

Charity suffereth long, *and* is kind; charity envieth not; charity vaunteth not itself, is not puffed up,

Doth not behave itself unseemly, seeketh not her own, is not easily provoked, thinketh no evil;

Rejoiceth not in iniquity, but rejoiceth in the truth;

Beareth all things, believeth all things, hopeth all things, endureth all things.

Charity never faileth: but whether *there be* prophecies, they shall fail; whether *there be* tongues, they shall cease; whether *there be* knowledge, it shall vanish away.

For we know in part, and we prophesy in part.

But when that which is perfect is come, then that which is in part shall be done away.

When I was a child, I spake as a child, I understood as a child, I thought as a child: but when I became a man, I put away childish things.

For now we see through a glass darkly; but then face to face: now I know in part; but then shall I know even as also I am known.

And now abideth faith, hope, charity, these three; but the greatest of these *is* charity [love].

I Corinthians 13

FORGIVENESS

A brother at Scetis committed a fault. A council was called to which Abba Moses was invited, but he refused to go. Then the priest sent someone to say to him, "Come, for everyone is waiting for you." So he got up and went, taking a leaking jug filled with water and carrying it with him. The other monks came out to meet him and said, "What is this, Father?" The old man replied: "My sins run out behind me and I do not see them, and today I am coming to judge the faults of another." When they heard that, they said no more to the brother but forgave him.

Desert Fathers

Monks, there are two kinds of immature people: those who do not see their own mistakes as mistakes, and those who do not forgive mistakes committed by someone else.

Anguttara Nikaya

As long as you cannot forgive the next man for being different, you are still far from the path of wisdom.

Chinese Wisdom

When Bankei held his seclusion weeks of meditation, pupils from many parts of Japan came to attend. During one of these gatherings, a pupil was caught stealing. The matter was reported to Bankei with the request that the culprit be expelled. Bankei ignored the case.

Later the pupil was caught in a similar act, and again Bankei disregarded the matter. This angered the other pupils, who drew up a petition asking for the dismissal of the thief, stating that otherwise they would leave in a body.

When Bankei had read the petition, he called everyone before him. "You are wise brothers," he told them. "You know what is right and what is wrong. You may go somewhere else to study if you wish, but this poor brother does not even know right from wrong. Who will teach him if I do not? I am going to keep him here even if all the rest of you leave."

A torrent of tears cleansed the face of the brother who had stolen. All desire to steal had vanished.

Sufi

It is great wisdom to know how to be silent and to look at neither the remarks, nor the deeds, nor the lives of others.

Saint John of the Cross

A monk was brought up before the brotherhood for having committed a grievous sin, and it was decided that he would be excommunicated. As the monk left the sanctuary, his head bent in shame, the esteemed Abba Bessarian stood up, fell into step behind his fellow monk and in a clear voice announced, "I, too, am a sinner."

Whatever is hurtful to you, do not do to any other person.

Moses

The Two Brothers

They told me the story of two monks who were blood brothers. The younger one had offended the older, and the older just could not forgive him. Every morning the younger one would knock on the door of his brother and call out, "Forgive me, Brother." But he would not. Day after day this went on, year after year.

After many years, the younger brother did not show up one morning. Nor the next, nor the next. The older one became uneasy. Finally, he went out to look for his brother. He knocked on every door. "Have you seen my brother?" No one had. He left the monastery, knocked on the doors of all the neighbors. "Have you seen my brother?" He kept going. Miles away from the monastery he would knock on a door. "Have you seen my brother?" People thought him strange, but he kept it up. Days went by, months, years. And that was all he had to say, except that when someone would show annoyance he would say, "Forgive me, Brother."

At last, after so many years of searching, he found himself back at his monastery. He knocked. The young Brother who answered did not recognize him, but was struck by the beauty of his face. He ran to call the others. They all came, crowding around. They were all struck by the beauty of this old man. Now some of the older ones recognized him. When they called out his name, he fell on his face. "Forgive me, Brothers," he said.

They wept, all of them.

Well, they made up a cell for him right beside the abbot's cell. And now, whenever any monk has difficulty forgiving his brother, why, he just slips in there for a few minutes. And guests can do the same.

Father Theophane

What you do not want done to yourself, do not do to others.

Confucius

❧❧❧❧❧❧❧❧

HUMILITY

❧❧❧❧❧❧❧❧

The Audacity of Humility

I walked up to an old, old monk and asked him, "What is the audacity of humility?" This man had never met me before, but do you know what his answer was? "To be the first to say 'I love you.'"

Father Theophane

❧❧❧❧❧❧❧❧

Lacking gold, a merchant is not a merchant, even though he may be very skillful in trading; similarly, lacking humility, a spiritual aspirant will never possess the joys of virtue, however great the confidence he places in his own intelligence.

Philokalia 3:38

❧❧❧❧❧❧❧❧

Pride

Do not boast that you have no pride, because it is less visible than an ant's foot on a black stone in a dark night.

And do not think that bringing it out from within is easy, for it is easier to extract a mountain from the earth with a needle.

Sufi

❧❧❧❧❧❧❧❧

Our most blessed Father Francis, wishing to teach Brother Masseo humility so that the manifold gifts the Most High had given him should increase the more, when the holy father was in retreat with his first truly holy companions, including Brother Masseo, said before the whole group: "Brother Masseo, all of these your companions have the grace of prayer and contemplation, but you have the grace of the Word of God to meet the needs of visitors. That is why, in order that they may be more free for prayer and contemplation, I wish you to be doorkeeper, almoner and have charge of the kitchen. When the brothers are at table you will eat outside the door so that, before visitors knock, you may satisfy them with a few words, so that no one need go outside but you. Do this in the name of sanctified obedience."

At this Brother Masseo immediately bowed his head and drew back his cowl and humbly obeyed. For several days he kept watch over door, alms and kitchen. But his companions, like men enlightened by God, became conscious of much inner strife of heart, because Brother Masseo was a man of great perfection and prayer as they were and more so, and yet the whole burden of the friary had been laid on him. So they asked the holy father to share out the duties among them for in no way could their consciences endure that the said brother should bear so many burdens. Further, they felt ineffectual in their prayers, and troubled in conscience unless Brother Masseo should be eased of his burdens.

Saint Francis, hearing this, agreed to the loving suggestions. He called Brother Masseo and said: "Brother Masseo, these your companions wish to take a share of the duties I have laid on you. I therefore wish the duties to be shared out." He humbly and patiently replied: "Father, whatever wholly or in part you lay upon me, I wholly consider it to be an act of God."

Then Saint Francis, observing their love and Brother Masseo's humility, gave a most wondrous sermon on holy humility, apart from which no virtue is acceptable in the eyes of God. He then shared out the duties and blessed all of them with the grace of the Holy Spirit. To the praise of God.

The substance of wealth is gold; of virtue, humility. Just as he who lacks gold is poor, even though this may not be outwardly apparent, so the spiritual aspirant who lacks humility is not virtuous.

Philokalia 3:38

Combine simplicity with self-control, and unite truth with humility, and you will keep house with justice, at whose table every other virtue likes to gather.

Philokalia 3:39

The Rebellion Against the Stomach

Once a man had a dream in which his hands and feet and mouth and brain all began to rebel against his stomach.

"You good-for-nothing sluggard!" the hands said. "We work all day long, sawing and hammering and lifting and carrying. By evening we're covered with blisters and scratches, and our joints ache, and we're covered with dirt. And meanwhile you just sit there, hogging all the food."

"We agree!" cried the feet. "Think how sore we get, walking back and forth all day long. And you just stuff yourself full, you greedy pig, so that you're that much heavier to carry about."

"That's right!" whined the mouth. "Where do you think all that food you love comes from? I'm the one who has to chew it all up, and as soon as I'm finished you suck it all down for yourself. Do you call that fair?"

"And what about me?" called the brain. "Do you think it's easy being up here, having to think about where your next meal is going to come from? And yet I get nothing at all for my pains."

And one by one the parts of the body joined the complaint against the stomach, which didn't say anything at all.

"I have an idea," the brain finally announced. "Let's all rebel against this lazy belly, and stop working for it."

"Superb idea!" all the other members and organs agreed. "We'll teach you how important we are, you pig. Then maybe you'll do a little work of your own."

So they all stopped working. The hands refused to do any lifting or carrying. The feet refused to walk. The mouth promised not to chew or swallow a single bite. And the brain swore it wouldn't come up with any more bright ideas. At first the stomach growled a bit, as it always did when it was hungry. But after a while it was quiet.

Then, to the dreaming man's surprise, he found he could not walk. He could not grasp anything in his hands. He could not even open his mouth. And he suddenly began to feel rather ill.

The dream seemed to go on for several days. As each day passed, the man felt worse and worse. "This rebellion had better not last much longer," he thought to himself, "or I'll starve."

Meanwhile, the hands and feet and mouth and brain just lay there, getting weaker and weaker. At first they roused themselves just enough to taunt the stomach every once in a while, but before long they didn't even have the energy for that.

Finally, the man heard a faint voice coming from the direction of his feet. "It could be that we were wrong," they were saying. "We suppose the stomach might have been working in his own way all along."

"I was just thinking the same thing," murmured the brain. "It's true he's been getting all the food. But it seems he's been sending most of it right back to us."

"We might as well admit our error," the mouth said. "The stomach has just as much work to do as the hands and feet and brain and teeth."

"Then let's all get back to work," they cried together. And at that the man woke up.

To his relief, he discovered his feet could walk again. His hands could grasp, his mouth could chew, and his brain could now think clearly. He began to feel much better.

"Well, there's a lesson for me," he thought as he filled his stomach at breakfast. "Either we all work together, or nothing works at all."

THE MIND

It is not only the slow rhythm of the walk but the rhythm with which the mind is moving: it is that rhythm with which the observation is gained which makes the difference between one person and another; it is that which brings about the harmony between one person and another.

The person who says, "I will not listen to your reason," no doubt has a reason, as everybody has a reason. But he could have a better reason still if he were able to listen and to understand the reason of another. The reason of a person's mind is just like making circles. One person's mind makes a circle in a minute; another person's mind makes a circle in five minutes: the reason is different. Another person's mind makes a circle in fifteen minutes; his reason is different again. The longer it takes, the wider is the horizon of his vision; and so is his outlook on life.

The Injustice of Mere Suspicion

A certain man lost an axe. He at once suspected the son of his neighbor had stolen it. When he saw the boy walking by, the boy looked like a fellow who had stolen an axe; when he listened to the boy's words, they sounded like those of a boy who had stolen an axe. All his actions and manners were those of a boy who had stolen an axe. Later, when digging a ditch, the man found the lost axe. The next day he saw again his neighbor's son, but in all the boy's manners and actions, there was nothing like a boy who had stolen an axe. The boy had not changed, but the man himself had changed! And the only reason for this change lay in his suspicion.

If I were to choose one sentence to sum up my whole philosophy, I should say: allow no evil in your thoughts.

Confucius

ৰৱৰৱৰৱৰৱৰৱ

When the ship of sinfulness is overwhelmed by the flood of tears, evil thoughts will react like people drowning in the waves and trying to grasp hold of something so as to keep afloat.

Philokalia 3:50

ৰৱৰৱৰৱৰৱৰৱ

The quest is an adventure as well as a journey: a work to be done and a study to be made, a blessing which gives hope and a burden of discipline which cannot be shirked.

Paul Brunton

ৰৱৰৱৰৱৰৱৰৱ

Guard your thoughts, words, and deeds. These three disciplines will speed you along the path to pure wisdom.

Dhammapada

ৰৱৰৱৰৱৰৱৰৱ

Use your body for doing good, not for harm. Train it to follow the dharma. Use your tongue for doing good, not for harm. Train it to speak kindly. Use your mind for doing good, not for harm. Train your mind in love. The wise are disciplined in body, speech, and mind. They are well controlled indeed.

Dhammapada

ৰৱৰৱৰৱৰৱৰৱ

Sa'di of Shiraz tells this story about himself:
When I was a child I was a pious boy, fervent in prayer and devotion. One night I was keeping vigil with my father, the Holy Koran on my lap.
Everyone else in the room began to slumber and soon was sound asleep, so

I said to my father, "None of these sleepers opens his eyes or raises his head to say his prayers. You would think that they were all dead."

My father replied, "My beloved son, I would rather you too were asleep like them than slandering."

Sufi

The Honest Disciple

Once a rabbi decided to test the honesty of his disciples, so he called them together and posed a question.

"What would you do if you were walking along and found a purse full of money lying in the road?" he asked.

"I'd return it to its owner," said one disciple.

"His answer comes so quickly, I must wonder if he really means it," the rabbi thought.

"I'd keep the money if nobody saw me find it," said another.

"He has a frank tongue, but a wicked heart," the rabbi told himself.

"Well, Rabbi," said a third disciple, "to be honest, I believe I'd be tempted to keep it. So I would pray to God that He give me the strength to resist such temptation and do the right thing."

"Aha!" thought the rabbi. "Here is the man I would trust."

Nothing is more unsettling than talkativeness and more pernicious than an unbridled tongue, disruptive as it is of the soul's proper state. For the soul's chatter destroys what we build each day and scatters what we have laboriously gathered together. What is more disastrous than this 'uncontrollable evil' (Jas. 3:8)? The tongue has to be restrained, checked by force and muzzled, so to speak, and made to serve only what is needful. Who can describe all the damage that the tongue does to the soul?

Philokalia 3:17

The music of life is in danger of being lost in the music of the voice.

Mahatma Gandhi

A man cannot utter two or three sentences without disclosing to intelligent ears precisely where he stands in life and thought, namely, whether in the kingdom of the senses . . . or in that of ideas . . . or in the realm of intuitions . . . . People seem not to see that their opinion of the world is also a confession of character. We can only see what we are . . .

Ralph Waldo Emerson

The true teacher identifies himself with his student and does not sit on a Himalayan height of self-esteem.

Paul Brunton

Like Calls to Like

Hasan of Basra went to see Rabia. She was sitting in the midst of a number of animals.
As soon as Hasan approached, they ran away.
Hasan said:
'Why did they do that?'
Rabia answered:
'You have been eating meat. All I had to eat was dry bread.'

Sufi

Thoughts gather about the soul according to its underlying quality: either they are like pirates and try to sink it, or they are like oarsmen and try to help it when it is in danger. The first tow it out into the open sea of sinful thoughts; the second steer it back to the nearest calm shore they can find.

Philokalia 3:50

Truth and Falsehood

Once upon a time Truth and Falsehood met each other on the road.
"Good afternoon," said Truth.

"Good afternoon," returned Falsehood. "And how are you doing these days?"

"Not very well at all, I'm afraid," sighed Truth. "The times are tough for a fellow like me, you know."

"Yes, I can see that," said Falsehood, glancing up and down at Truth's ragged clothes. "You look like you haven't had a bite to eat in quite some time."

"To be honest, I haven't," admitted Truth. "No one seems to want to employ me nowadays. Wherever I go, most people ignore me or mock me. It's getting discouraging, I can tell you. I'm beginning to ask myself why I put up with it."

"And why the devil do you? Come with me, and I'll show you how to get along. There's no reason in the world why you can't stuff yourself with as much as you want to eat, like me, and dress in the finest clothes, like me. But you must promise not to say a word against me while we're together."

So Truth promised and agreed to go along with Falsehood for awhile, not because he liked his company so much, but because he was so hungry he thought he'd faint soon if he didn't get something into his stomach. They walked down the road until they came to a city, and Falsehood at once led the way to the very best table at the very best restaurant.

"Waiter, bring us your choicest meats, your sweetest sweets, your finest wine!" he called, and they ate and drank all afternoon. At last, when they could hold no more, Falsehood began banging his fist on the table and calling for the manager, who came running at once.

"What the devil kind of place is this?" Falsehood snapped. "I gave that waiter a gold piece nearly an hour ago, and he still hasn't brought our change."

The manager summoned the waiter, who said he'd never even seen a penny out of the gentleman.

"What?" Falsehood shouted, so that everyone in the place turned and looked. "I can't believe this place! Innocent, law-abiding citizens come in to eat, and you rob them of their hard-earned money! You're a pack of thieves and liars! You may have fooled me once, but you'll never see me again! Here!" He threw a gold piece at the manager. "Now this time bring me my change!"

But the manager, fearing his restaurant's reputation would suffer, refused to take the gold piece, and instead brought Falsehood change for the first gold piece he claimed to have spent. Then he took the waiter aside and called him a scoundrel, and said he had a mind to fire him. And as much as the waiter protested that he'd never collected a cent from the man, the manager refused to believe him.

"Oh Truth, where have you hidden yourself?" the waiter sighed. "Have you now deserted even us hard-working souls?"

"No, I'm here," Truth groaned to himself, "but my judgment gave way to my hunger, and now I can't speak up without breaking my promise to Falsehood."

As soon as they were on the street, Falsehood gave a hearty laugh and slapped Truth on the back. "You see how the world works?" he cried. "I managed it all quite well, don't you think?"

But Truth slipped from his side.

"I'd rather starve than live as you do," he said.

And so Truth and Falsehood went their separate ways, and never traveled together again.

Grecian Folktale

Let no one think lightly of evil and say to himself, "Sorrow will not come to me." Little by little a person becomes evil, as a water pot is filled by drops of water. Let no one think lightly of good and say to himself, "Joy will not come to me." Little by little a person becomes good, as a water pot is filled by drops of water.

Dhammapada

Be vigilant; guard your mind against negative thoughts.

Guatama Buddha

That the birds of worry and care fly above your
Head, this you cannot change,
But that they build nests in your hair,
This you can prevent.

Chinese Proverb

By love may He be gotten and holden, by thought never.

The Cloud of Unknowing

Reason is like an officer when the King appears. The officer then loses his power and hides himself. Reason is the shadow cast by God; God is the sun.

Jalaluddin Rumi

Look sharply after your thoughts. They come unlooked for, like a new bird seen on your trees, and, if you turn to your usual task, they disappear, and you shall never find that perception again.

Ralph Waldo Emerson

A man who does not learn from life grows old like an ox: his body grows, but not his wisdom.

Dhammapada

Someone Sees You

Once upon a time a man decided to sneak into his neighbor's fields and steal some wheat. "If I take just a little from each field, no one will notice," he told himself, "but it will all add up to a nice pile of wheat for me." So he waited for the darkest night, when thick clouds lay over the moon, and he crept out of his house. He took his youngest daughter with him.

"Daughter," he whispered, "you must stand guard, and call out if anyone sees me."

The man stole into the first field to begin reaping, and before long the child called out, "Father, someone sees you!"

The man looked all around, but he saw no one, so he gathered his stolen wheat and moved on to a second field.

"Father, someone sees you!" the child cried again.

The man stopped and looked all around, but once again he saw no one. He gathered more wheat, and moved to a third field.

A little while passed, and the daughter cried out, "Father, someone sees you!"

Once more the man stopped his work and looked in every direction, but he saw no one at all, so he bundled his wheat and crept into the last field.

"Father, someone sees you!" the child called again.

The man stopped his reaping, looked all around, and once again saw no one. "Why in the world do you keep saying someone sees me?" he angrily asked his daughter. "I've looked everywhere, and I don't see anyone."

"Father," murmured the child, "Someone sees you from above."

Adopt the pace of nature, her secret is patience.

Ralph Waldo Emerson

❧☙❧☙❧☙❧☙❧☙❧☙

How poor are they that have not patience!
What wound did ever heal but by degrees?

William Shakespeare

❧☙❧☙❧☙❧☙❧☙❧☙

An elder said: The reason why we do not get anywhere is that we do not know our limits, and we are not patient in carrying on the work we have begun. But without any labour at all we want to gain possession of virtue.

Desert Fathers

❧☙❧☙❧☙❧☙❧☙❧☙

God doth not need
Either man's work or his own gifts. Who best
Bear his mild yoke, they serve him best. His state
Is kingly: thousands at his bidding speed,
And post o'er land and ocean without rest;
They also serve who only stand and wait.

Milton, *Paradise Lost*

❧☙❧☙❧☙❧☙❧☙❧☙

SERVICE

❧☙❧☙❧☙❧☙❧☙❧☙

What Do They Need?

There's a monk there who will never give you advice, but only a question. I was told his questions could be very helpful. I sought him out. "I am a parish priest," I said. "I'm here on retreat. Could you give me a question?"

"Ah, yes," he answered. "My question is, 'What do they need?' "

I came away disappointed. I spent a few hours with the question, writing out answers, but finally I went back to him.

"Excuse me. Perhaps I didn't make myself clear. Your question has been helpful, but I wasn't so much interested in thinking about my apostolate during this retreat. Rather I wanted to think seriously about my own spiritual life. Could you give me a question for my own spiritual life?"

"Ah, I see. Then my question is, 'What do they REALLY need?' "

Father Theophane

ё▟ё▟ё▟ё▟ё▟ё▟ё▟

Our Lady's Juggler

In the days of King Louis there was a poor juggler in France, a native of Compiègne, Barnaby by name, who went about from town to town performing feats of skill and strength.

On fair days he would unfold an old worn-out carpet in the public square, and when by means of a jovial address, which he had learned of a very ancient juggler, and which he never varied in the least, he had drawn together the children and loafers, he assumed extraordinary attitudes, and balanced a tin plate on the tip of his nose. At first the crowd would feign indifference.

But when, supporting himself on his hands face downward, he threw into the air six copper balls, which glittered in the sunshine, and caught them again with his feet; or when throwing himself backward until his heels and the nape of the neck met, giving his body the form of a perfect wheel, he would juggle in this posture with a dozen knives, a murmur of admiration would escape the spectators, and pieces of money [would] rain down upon the carpet.

Nevertheless, like the majority of those who live by their wits, Barnaby of Compiègne had a great struggle to make a living.

Earning his bread by the sweat of his brow, he bore rather more than his share of the penalties consequent upon the misdoings of our father Adam.

Again, he was unable to work as constantly as he would have been willing to do. The warmth of the sun and the broad daylight were as necessary to enable him to display his brilliant parts as to the trees if flower and fruit should be expected of them. In wintertime he was nothing more than a tree stripped of its leaves, and as it were dead. The frozen ground was hard to the juggler, and, like the grasshopper of which Marie de France tells us, the inclement season caused him to suffer both cold and hunger. But as he was simple-natured he bore his ills patiently.

He had never meditated on the origin of wealth, nor upon the inequality of human conditions. He believed firmly that if this life should prove hard, the life to come could not fail to redress the balance, and this hope upheld him. He did not resemble those thievish and miscreant Merry Andrews who sell their souls to the devil. He never blasphemed God's name; he lived uprightly, and although he had no wife of his own, he did not covet his neighbor's, since woman is ever the enemy of the strong man, as it appears by the history of Samson recorded in the Scriptures.

In truth, his was not a nature much disposed to carnal delights, and it was a greater deprivation to him to forsake the tankard than the Hebe who bore it. For whilst not wanting in sobriety, he was fond of a drink when the weather waxed hot. He was a worthy man who feared God, and was very devoted to the Blessed Virgin.

Never did he fail on entering a church to fall upon his knees before the image of the Mother of God, and offer up this prayer to her:

"Blessed Lady, keep watch over my life until it shall please God that I die, and when I am dead, ensure to me the possession of the joys of paradise."

Now on a certain evening after a dreary wet day, as Barnaby pursued his road, sad and bent, carrying under his arm his balls and knives wrapped up in his old carpet, on the watch for some barn where, though he might not sup, he might sleep, he perceived on the road, going in the same direction as himself, a monk, whom he saluted courteously. And as they walked at the same rate they fell into conversation with one another.

"Fellow traveler," said the monk, "how comes it about that you are clothed all in green? Is it perhaps in order to take the part of a jester in some mystery play?"

"Not at all, good father," replied Barnaby. "Such as you see me, I am called Barnaby, and for my calling I am a juggler. There would be no pleasanter calling in the world if it would always provide one with daily bread."

"Friend Barnaby," returned the monk, "be careful what you say. There is no calling more pleasant than the monastic life. Those who lead it are occupied with the praises of God, the Blessed Virgin, and the saints; and, indeed, the religious life is one ceaseless hymn to the Lord."

Barnaby replied—

"Good father, I own that I spoke like an ignorant man. Your calling cannot be in any respect compared to mine, and although there may be some merit in dancing with a penny balanced on a stick on the tip of one's nose, it is not a merit which comes within hail of your own. Gladly would I, like you, good father, sing my office day by day, and especially the office of the most Holy Virgin, to whom I have vowed a singular devotion. In order to embrace the monastic life I would willingly abandon the art by which from Soissons to Beauvais I am well known in upward of six hundred towns and villages."

The monk was touched by the juggler's simplicity, and as he was not lacking in discernment, he at once recognized in Barnaby one of those men of whom it is said in the Scriptures: Peace on earth to men of good will. And for this reason he replied—

"Friend Barnaby, come with me, and I will have you admitted into the monastery of which I am prior. He who guided St. Mary of Egypt in the desert set me upon your path to lead you into the way of salvation."

It was in this manner, then, that Barnaby became a monk. In the monastery into which he was received the religious vied with one another in the worship of the Blessed Virgin, and in her honor each employed all the knowledge and all the skill which God had given him.

The prior on his part wrote books dealing according to the rules of scholarship with the virtues of the Mother of God.

Brother Maurice, with a deft hand, copied out these treatises upon sheets of vellum.

Brother Alexander adorned the leaves with delicate miniature paintings. Here were displayed the Queen of Heaven seated upon Solomon's throne, and while four lions were on guard at her feet, around the nimbus which encircled her head hovered seven doves, which are the seven gifts of the Holy Spirit, the gifts, namely, of Fear, Piety, Knowledge, Strength, Counsel, Understanding, and Wisdom. For her companions she had six virgins with hair of gold, namely, Humility, Prudence, Seclusion, Submission, Virginity, and Obedience.

At her feet were two little naked figures, perfectly white, in an attitude of supplication. These were souls imploring her all-powerful intercession for their soul's health, and we may be sure not imploring in vain.

Upon another page facing this, Brother Alexander represented Eve, so that the Fall and the Redemption could be perceived at one and the same time—Eve the Wife abased, and Mary the Virgin exalted.

Furthermore, to the marvel of the beholder, this book contained present-ments of the Well of Living Waters, the Fountain, the Lily, the Moon, the Sun, and the Garden Enclosed of which the Song of Songs tells us, the Gate of Heaven and the City of God, and all these things were symbols of the Blessed Virgin.

Brother Marbode was likewise one of the most loving children of Mary.

He spent all his days carving images in stone, so that his beard, his eye-brows, and his hair were white with dust, and his eyes continually swollen and weeping; but his strength and cheerfulness were not diminished, although he was now well gone in years, and it was clear that the Queen of Paradise still cherished her servant in his old age. Marbode represented her seated upon a throne, her brow encircled with an orb-shaped nimbus set with pearls. And he took care that the folds of her dress should cover the feet of her, concerning whom the prophet declared: My beloved is as a garden enclosed.

Sometimes, too, he depicted her in the semblance of a child full of grace, and appearing to say, "Thou art my God, even from my mother's womb."

In the priory, moreover, were poets who composed hymns in Latin, both in prose and verse, in honor of the Blessed Virgin Mary, and amongst the company was even a brother from Picardy who sang the miracles of Our Lady in rhymed verse and in the vulgar tongue.

Being a witness of this emulation in praise and the glorious harvest of their labors, Barnaby mourned his own ignorance and simplicity.

"Alas!" he sighed, as he took his solitary walk in the little shelterless garden of the monastery, "wretched sight that I am, to be unable, like my brothers, worthily to praise the Holy Mother of God, to whom I have vowed my whole heart's affection. Alas! Alas! I am but a rough man and unskilled in the arts, and I can render you in service, blessed Lady, neither edifying ser-mons, nor treatises set out in order according to rule, nor ingenious paintings, nor statues truthfully sculptured, nor verses whose march is measured to the beat of feet. No gift have I, alas!"

After this fashion he groaned and gave himself up to sorrow. But one evening, when the monks were spending their hour of liberty in conversation, he heard one of them tell the tale of a religious man who could repeat nothing other than the Ave Maria. This poor man was despised for his ignorance; but after his death there issued forth from his mouth five roses in honor of the five letters of the name Maria, and thus his sanctity was made manifest.

Whilst he listened to this narrative Barnaby marveled yet once again at the loving kindness of the Virgin; but the lesson of that blessed death did not avail to console him, for his heart overflowed with zeal, and he longed to advance the glory of his Lady, who is in heaven.

How to compass this he sought but could find no way, and day by day he became the more cast down, when one morning he awakened filled full with joy, hastened to the chapel, and remained there alone for more than an hour. After dinner he returned to the chapel once more.

And, starting from that moment, he repaired daily to the chapel at such hours as it was deserted, and spent within it a good part of the time which the other monks devoted to the liberal and mechanical arts. His sadness vanished, nor did he any longer groan.

A demeanor so strange awakened the curiosity of the monks.

These began to ask one another for what purpose Brother Barnaby could be indulging so persistently in retreat.

The prior, whose duty it is to let nothing escape him in the behavior of his children in religion, resolved to keep a watch over Barnaby during his withdrawals to the chapel. One day, then, when he was shut up there after his custom, the prior, accompanied by two of the older monks, went to discover through the chinks in the door what was going on within the chapel.

They saw Barnaby before the altar of the Blessed Virgin, head downward, with his feet in the air, and he was juggling with six balls of copper and a dozen knives. In honor of the Holy Mother of God he was performing those feats, which aforetime had won him most renown. Not recognizing that the simple fellow was thus placing at the service of the Blessed Virgin his knowledge and skill, the two old monks exclaimed against the sacrilege.

The prior was aware how stainless was Barnaby's soul, but he concluded that he had been seized with madness. They were all three preparing to lead him swiftly from the chapel, when they saw the Blessed Virgin descend the steps of the altar and advance to wipe away with a fold of her azure robe the sweat which was dropping from her juggler's forehead.

Then the prior, falling upon his face upon the pavement, uttered these words—

"Blessed are the simplehearted, for they shall see God."

"Amen!" responded the old brethren, and kissed the ground.

Anatole France

What is the essence of life? To serve others and to do good.

Aristotle

❧❧❧❧❧❧❧

The vocation of every man and woman is to serve other people.

Leo Tolstoy

❧❧❧❧❧❧❧

There is joy in transcending self to serve others.

Mother Teresa

❧❧❧❧❧❧❧

The young salesman approached the farmer and began to talk excitedly about the book he was carrying. "This book will tell you everything you need to know about farming," the young man said enthusiastically. "It tells you when to sow and when to reap. It tells you about weather, what to expect and when to expect it. This book tells you all you need to know."

"Young man," the farmer said, "that's not the problem. I know everything that is in that book. My problem is doing it."

Retold by Joseph Gosse

❧❧❧❧❧❧❧

Doing nothing for others is the undoing of ourselves.

Benjamin Franklin

❧❧❧❧❧❧❧

Q: *What can a little person like me do for peace?*
A: To the millions who live in this world today let me say that there are many worthwhile things little people can do, both individually and collectively. When I dedicated my life to be of as much service as possible to my fellow human beings someone said to me very sarcastically, "What do you think you can do?" And I replied, "I know I am a little person and can do only little things, but there are so many little things that need to be done." And I never had any trouble finding worthwhile little things to do. When I started my pilgrimage I was asking for very big things and someone said to me then, "You might as well ask for the moon." But I answered, "If enough of us little people ask together even very, very big things will be granted."

I can say this to you: Live the present. Do the things you know need to be done. Do all the good you can each day. The future will unfold.

Peace Pilgrim

ع&ع&ع&ع&ع&ع&

Do all the good you can, to all the people you can, for as long as you can.

John Wesley

ع&ع&ع&ع&ع&ع&

When I see people very anxious to know what sort of prayer they practise, covering their faces and afraid to move or think, lest they should lose any slight tenderness and devotion they feel, I know how little they understand how to obtain union with God since they think it consists in such things as these.

No, sisters, no; our Lord expects *works* from us. If you see a sick sister whom you can relieve, never fear losing your devotion: treat her with compassion; if she is in pain, feel for it as if it were your own, and when there is need, fast so that she may eat. This is the true union of our will with the will of God. If someone else is well spoken of, be more pleased than if it were yourself; this is easy enough, for if you were humble it would vex you to be praised. It is a great good to rejoice in your sister's virtues being known and to feel as sorry for the fault you see in her as if it were yours, hiding it from the sight of others.

The Life of St. Teresa

ع&ع&ع&ع&ع&ع&

No one has a right to sit down and feel hopeless. There's too much work to do.

Dorothy Day

ع&ع&ع&ع&ع&ع&

To be right, a person must do one of two things: either he must learn to have God in his work and hold fast to Him there, or he must give up his work altogether. Since, however, man cannot live without activities that are both human and various, we must learn to keep God in everything we do, and whatever the job or place, keep on with Him, letting nothing stand in our way.

Meister Eckhart

Living creatures are nourished by food, and food is nourished by rain; rain itself is the water of life, which comes from selfless worship and service.

Sri Krishna, *Bhagavad Gita*

What a man does here and now with holy intent is no less important, no less a true link with the divine being than the life in the world to come.

Martin Buber

That he had been lately sent into Burgundy, to buy the provision of wine for the society, which was a very unwelcome task for him, because he had no turn for business and because he was lame, and could not go about the boat but by rolling himself over the casks. That however he gave himself no uneasiness about it, nor about the purchase of the wine. That he said to God, it was His business he was about, and that he afterwards found it very well performed. That he had been sent into Auvergne the year before upon the same account; that he could not tell how the matter passed, but that it proved very well.

So likewise, in his business in the kitchen (to which he had naturally a great aversion), having accustomed himself to do everything there for the love of God, and with prayer, upon all occasions, for His grace to do the work well, he had found everything easy, during the fifteen years that he had been employed there.

That he was very well pleased with the post he was now in; but that he was as ready to quit that as the former, since he was always pleasing himself in every condition, by doing little things for the love of God.

The Practice of the Presence of God

Every good act is charity.
A man's true wealth hereafter is
the good that he does in this world
for his fellow man.

Mohammed

✄✄✄✄✄✄✄

Only a life lived for others is a life worthwhile.

Albert Einstein

✄✄✄✄✄✄✄

Do not close your eyes before suffering. Find ways to be with those who are suffering by all means, including personal contact and visits, images, sound. By such means, awaken yourself and others to the reality of suffering in the world.

Guatama Buddha

✄✄✄✄✄✄✄

You say nothing is created new? Don't worry about it. With the mud of the earth, make a cup from which your brother can drink.

Antonio Machado

✄✄✄✄✄✄✄

When one reaches out to help another he touches the face of God.

Walt Whitman

✄✄✄✄✄✄✄

If I am not for myself, who is for me? But if I am only for myself, what am I?

Hillel

✄✄✄✄✄✄✄

One of the elders had finished his baskets and had already put handles on them, when he heard his neighbour saying: What shall I do? The market is about to begin and I have nothing with which to make handles for my baskets? At once the elder went in and took off his handles, giving them to the brother with the words: Here, I don't need these, take them and put them on your baskets. Thus in his great charity he saw to it that his brother's work was finished while his own remained incomplete.

Desert Fathers

❦❧❦❧❦❧❦❧❦❧❦❧

If someone takes your coat, give him your cloak as well; if he makes you go a mile with him, go with him two.

The Gospel According to Saint Matthew

❦❧❦❧❦❧❦❧❦❧❦❧

No act of kindness, no matter how small, is ever wasted.

Aesop

❦❧❦❧❦❧❦❧❦❧❦❧

Small service is true service . . . .
The daisy, by the shadow that it casts,
Protects the lingering dewdrop from the sun.

William Wordsworth

❦❧❦❧❦❧❦❧❦❧❦❧

If someone needs our help
it is our special duty to provide it
to the utmost of our power.

Marcus Tullius Cicero

❦❧❦❧❦❧❦❧❦❧❦❧

'As to how ye are to carry the religious teachings into practice in your everyday life, bear in mind the following: some there may be among you who are proud of their apparent sanctity, but who, at heart, are really devoted to acquiring name and fame in this world; they dispense a hundred necessary and unnecessary things in charity, hoping thereby to reap a liberal return. This, though displeasing to the divinities gifted with divine vision, is persevered in by selfish beings of obscured vision. The hypocrisy of thus hankering after the rich juices of this world, while outwardly appearing pious and devout, because unable to face the ridicule of the world is like partaking of delicacies and rich food mixed with deadly aconite. Therefore, drink not the venom of desire for worldly fame and name; but casting aside all the fetters of worldly duties, which but lead to this desire, devote yourselves to sincere and earnest devotion.'

The disciples then inquired if they could engage in worldly duties, in a small way, for the benefit of others, and he said: 'If there be not the least self-interest attached to such duties, it is permissible. But such detachment is indeed rare; and works performed for the good of others seldom succeed if not wholly freed from self-interest. Even without seeking to benefit others, it is with difficulty that works done even in one's own interest are successful. It is as if a man helplessly drowning were to try to save another man in the same predicament. One should not be over-anxious and hasty in setting out to serve others before one hath oneself realized Truth in its fullness; to be so, would be like the blind leading the blind. As long as the sky endureth, so long will there be no end of sentient beings for one to serve; and to everyone cometh the opportunity for such service. Till the opportunity comes, I exhort each of you to have but the one resolve, namely, to attain Buddhahood for the good of all living things.'

Evans-Wentz, *Tibet's Great Yogi, Milarepa*

SPIRITUAL DIRECTION

Indian Religion

"Indian religion is as old as the Creator. In our way of life the Elders give spiritual direction. The wisdom of thousands of years flows through their lips. Others want to learn what our Elders know. They find some carnival chief who'll give them a sweat bath for $250, and then they think they know all about Indian religion. But you don't sell the religion of your people. Our ceremonies and our religion are not for sale . . . ."

Mathew King, Native American Elder/Lakota

If you see a wise man who steers you away from the wrong path, follow him as you would one who can reveal hidden treasures. Only good can come out of it.

Dhammapada

It is usually quite impossible for the average aspirant to determine who is a fully qualified master. But it is sometimes quite possible to determine who is *not* a master. He may apply this negative test to the supposed master's personal conduct and public teaching. If a man claims to have attained the fullness of his higher being, we may test his claim by the moral fruits he shows. For he ought constantly to exercise the qualities of compassion, self-restraint, nonattachment, and calmness on the positive side and freedom from malice, backbiting, greed, lust and anger on the negative side.

Paul Brunton

He who has dedicated his life to this kind of service will find before long that others come to him—perhaps a few at first, but later many more—to pile on his sturdy shoulders the burdens and sufferings, the perplexities and gropings which they find so difficult to deal with themselves.

Paul Brunton

Keeping company with the immature is like going on a long journey with an enemy. The company of the wise is joyful, like reunion with one's family. Therefore, live among the wise, who are understanding, patient, responsible, and noble. Keep their company like the moon moving among the stars.

Dhammapada

When the King visited the monasteries of the great Zen master Lin Chi, he was astonished to learn that there were more than ten thousand monks living there with him.

Wanting to know the exact number of monks, the King asked, "How many disciples do you have?"

Lin Chi replied, "Four or five at the very most."

Zen

ཙ⌇ཙ⌇ཙ⌇ཙ⌇ཙ

Some people want to see God with their eyes as they see a cow, and to love Him as they love their cow—for the milk and cheese and profit it brings them. This is how it is with people who love God for the sake of outward wealth or inward comfort.

Meister Eckhart

ཙ⌇ཙ⌇ཙ⌇ཙ⌇ཙ

Everywhere man blames nature and fate, yet his fate is mostly but the echo of his character and passions, his mistakes and weaknesses.

Democritus

ཙ⌇ཙ⌇ཙ⌇ཙ⌇ཙ

"I want to learn to swim."

"Do you want to make a bargain about it?"

"No. I only have to take my ton of cabbage."

"What cabbage?"

"The food which I will need on the other island."

"There is better food there."

"I don't know what you mean. I cannot be sure. I must take my cabbage."

"You cannot swim, for one thing, with a ton of cabbage."

"Then I cannot go. You call it a load. I call it my essential nutrition."

"Suppose, as an allegory, we say not 'cabbage,' but 'assumptions,' or 'destructive ideas'?"

"I am going to take my cabbage to some instructor who understands my needs."

Sufi

ཙ⌇ཙ⌇ཙ⌇ཙ⌇ཙ

When you see a worthy person,
Endeavor to emulate him,

When you see an unworthy person,
Then examine your inner self.

Confucius

❧❧❧❧❧❧❧

The first and best victory is to conquer self; to be conquered by self is, of all things, the most shameful and vile.

Plato

❧❧❧❧❧❧❧

Thou wast seeking what thou shouldest offer in thy behalf; offer thyself. For what doth God ask of thee, except thyself? Since in the whole earthly creation He made nothing better than thee.

Saint Augustine

❧❧❧❧❧❧❧

To be a Sufi is to cease from taking trouble; and there is no greater trouble for thee than thine own self, for when thou art occupied with thyself, thou remainest away from God.

Abu Sa'id

❧❧❧❧❧❧❧

Each of us has within us a Mother Teresa and a Hitler. It is up to us to choose what we want to be.

Elisabeth Kübler-Ross

❧❧❧❧❧❧❧

When warriors are leaders, you will have war. We must raise leaders of peace. We must unite the religions of the world as the spiritual force strong enough to prevail in peace.

It is no longer good enough to cry *peace*. We must act *peace*, live *peace*, and march in *peace* in alliance with the people of the world.

We are the spiritual energy that is thousands of times stronger than nuclear energy. Our energy is the combined will of *all* people with the spirit of the Natural World, to be of one body, one heart, and one mind for *peace*.

Tadodaho Chief Leon Shenandoah Haudenosaunee
The Six Nations Iroquois Confederacy, October 25, 1985

He who understands others
　　Is learned.
He who knows himself
　　Is wise.
He who conquers others
　　Has muscular strength,
He who subdues himself
　　Is strong.
He who is content,
　　Is wealthy,
He who does not lose
　　His soul
Will endure.

Lao-Tse

Once I looked at my murshid and there came to my inquisitive mind a thought, "Why should a great soul such as my murshid wear gold-embroidered slippers?" But I checked myself at once, and it was only a thought. It could never have escaped my lips; it was under control. But there it was known. I could not cover my insolence with my lips; my heart was open before my murshid as an open book. He instantly saw into it and read my thought. And do you know what answer he gave me? He said, "The treasures of the earth I have at my feet."

Sufi, retold by Hazrat Inayat Khan

A master issues no command and requires no obedience. Others may do so but not he.

Paul Brunton

Better than performing a thousand rituals month by month for a hundred years is a moment's homage to one living in wisdom. Better than tending the sacrificial fire in the forest for a thousand years is a moment's homage to one living in wisdom.

Dhammapada

They are not following dharma who resort to violence to achieve their purpose. But those who lead others through nonviolent means, knowing right and wrong, may be called guardians of the dharma.

Guatama Buddha

I went to the woods because I wished to live deliberately, to front only the essential facts of life, and see if I could not learn what it had to teach, and not, when I came to die, discover that I had not lived.

Henry David Thoreau

Once there was a disciple of a Greek philosopher who was commanded by his Master for three years to give money to everyone who insulted him. When this period of trial was over, the Master said to him: Now you can go to Athens and learn wisdom. When the disciple was entering Athens he met a certain wise man who sat at the gate insulting everybody who came and went. He also insulted the disciple who immediately burst out laughing. Why do you laugh when I insult you? said the wise man. Because, said the disciple, for three years I have been paying for this kind of thing and now you give it to me for nothing. Enter the city, said the wise man, it is all yours.

Desert Fathers

There are many people in the world who are poor in spirit, but not in the way that they should be; there are many who mourn, but for some financial loss or the death of their children; many are gentle, but towards unclean passions; many hunger and thirst, but only to seize what does not belong to them and to profit from injustice; many are merciful, but towards their bodies and the things that serve the body; many are pure in heart, but for the sake of self-esteem; many are peace-makers, but by making the soul submit to the flesh; many are persecuted, but as wrongdoers; many are reviled, but for shameful sins. Only those are blessed who do or suffer these things for the sake of Christ and after His example. Why? Because theirs is the kingdom of heaven, and they shall see God (cf. Matt. 5:3-12). It is not because they do or suffer these things that they are blessed, for those of whom we have spoken above do the same; it is because they do them and suffer them for the sake of Christ and after His example.

Philokalia 2:90

In addition to voluntary suffering, you must also accept that which comes against your will—I mean slander, material losses and sickness. For if you do not accept these but rebel against them, you are like someone who wants to eat his bread only with honey, never with salt. Such a man does not always have pleasure as his companion, but always has nausea as his neighbour.

Philokalia 3:39

Now you may ask, How can we come to perceive this direct leading of God? By a careful looking at home, and abiding within the gates of thy own soul. Therefore, let a man be at home in his own heart, and cease from his restless chase of and search after outward things.

Johannes Tauler

Part III

Ascent of the
Mountain of Truth

Ascent of the Mountain of Truth

The Mountain of Decision

"How long have you been a monk?" I asked.

"A real monk? Not long. It took me fifty years to get up the Mountain of Decision."

"Do you have to see first before you decide, or is it that you decide first and then you see?"

"If you'll take my advice," he said, "You'll drop the questions, and go right up the mountain."

Father Theophane

To ascend the Mountain of Truth is to scale the highest reaches of consciousness to the heart of existence. En route we cross the rocky steeps of self-will and pass through shadows of desires in a landscape colored by changing thoughts, feelings, beliefs, opinions, constructs about God, and immature ways of seeing. It is a rite of passage born of our first priority—*to love God above all else.*

Initially, however, love is enkindled through the practice of virtue, through self-discipline. Later the practice of virtue arises from the sacred fire of love itself, not from the disciplines of realization. But between levels of awareness, the journey is repetitive as if love is dragging its feet to our destination. When problems are no longer challenges, only changing scenes in the landscape of life, the journey moves to another level. Eventually, we experience an uninterrupted awareness of God that is beyond swarming thoughts and scattered activities. Such an ever-constant awareness of God is the Supreme Ambition, the ambition beyond ambition.

The ascent of the Holy Mountain—the passage through consciousness to our deepest center wherein we live in unity with God—is the ultimate "higher education." The truth is learned without learning. To see a grain of sand is to see all possible worlds. To see a drop of water is to see the nature of all water. To see the sun is to experience the birth of the universe with its planets and moons and stars.

Spiritual education is not knowledge but wisdom, not information but inspiration. *Our textbook is the illumined life.* Its pages shine with celestial light on which are recorded our spiritual heritage and destiny. Ancient questions are asked, then answered: Who am I? What is the purpose of life? What is the nature of human beings? What is our highest potential? What is the purpose of suffering? What is death? How can we be at peace in a world of ceaseless turmoil and changing circumstances?

In convents and monasteries, in "forest academies," and in secluded mystery schools, pilgrims of the quest have sought Truth. Travelers East and West have entered the silent inner sanctuary of the heart to seek the pearl of great price, that which has been within us all the time. The path to this world of love, wisdom, unselfishness, and compassion is revealed in the harmonies of sacred scriptures. Blind to our hidden Self, we embrace the world religions as a staff to lean upon as we begin our climb up the Holy Mountain.

We have been in exile, lost in the midst of our own fears, pacing the wilderness of the world when what we seek is the hidden Self clothed in silence. The quest is a Homecoming where we are offered the cup of Wisdom. To drink deeply of its living water results in a complete transformation of consciousness.

Will we drink? Our illuminated textbook of "higher education" reveals that emptiness is fullness, death is birth, the *will* is the key to spiritual wisdom. Wherever our desire is, so is our will. When the will pursues its proper developmental direction and seeks the Divine, we shall drink.

Stories in the third section reveal what occurs as we drink from the cup of Wisdom, then undergo an inner transformation which affects our whole being—will, character, conduct, consciousness.

Like the caterpillar which undergoes a spectacular metamorphosis, we are born anew—a new woman, a new man. The caterpillar is symbolic of a life governed by our self-centered nature, when we flirt with our selfish cravings, tripping over the rocks and stones which litter our path. Initially, we are on the outskirts of consciousness not ready to enter unknown depths, but then we awaken from the shadows of our yearnings to seek God. Through meditation and discipline we withdraw to the harbor of our soul where we experience the grace of both dryness and inpourings of light.

After we reach the limits of what we can do, when it seems that we live between the shores of heaven and earth, the Divine initiates a sudden, irreversible breakthrough deep in our unconscious, revealing our union. Now purification and the unfolding of our potential are directed by the Divine alone. In Christianity, this is the beginning of the "dark night of the spirit" and the unitive state of consciousness. It is a point of no return. The caterpillar enters the cocoon to begin a passage which contemplative literature calls "transforming union," a journey inward and downward to the depths of being. This passive night of the spirit is the falling away of the ego-center (self-will), a state of possession by God in which our deepest union is revealed. No longer a glimpse of unity, it is a permanent state of consciousness.

Within the heart of God, in a cocoon of light which looks dark, the caterpillar undergoes her metamorphosis to emerge under His direction as a spectacular butterfly. In this new stage of growth, she experiences her greatest human potential, enormous energy, love, creativity, and heightened intelligence. "The soul is sensitive, loyal, gentle, kind, self-giving—the abundant life resulting from the Divine at work in her soul." She is God's unitive partner giving herself away in selfless acts of charity. On wings of light, the soul wraps the suffering of the world in compassion. It is her destiny born of deep joy; she could not do otherwise. Then, after long years in the full unitive state in which she gives herself completely away, a new phase of life begins.

In today's world, peace will not come from an avalanche of new ideas but from this profound change in the human heart. When we spiritually grow up and experience such a deep transformation of consciousness, we no longer slumber unaware of the effects of our actions, thoughts, and words. We are no longer blind to the vanity of our day. Our eyes open to eternity; our words become a psalm; our heart, wet with the dew of heaven, pours love and compassion wherever there is need.

From the distant summit of the Holy Mountain, we see the quest in retrospect. The landscape, once marked by changing thoughts, emotions, immature expectations, and beliefs, is now colored in love.

Stories in the *Ascent of the Mountain of Truth* can inspire us in our journey of the heart. In *The Ascent*, we discover the singleness of purpose required for self-mastery. The road of the senses leads us under the razor-sharp hooves of desire and sorrow. The path of spiritual development is less-traveled but leads us Home. As we read this chapter, may we consider loving the questions with an open heart. What joy do we seek in the circumstances of life that can only be met from within our own being? What is the deepest prayer of our heart? How can the will be strengthened to follow its higher purpose? How much do we give to moments of meditation, prayer, openness to nature? Can we allow space and compassion for our changing seasons of the heart, for others to change, for relationships to change?

In *Transformation of Consciousness*, we discover stories of illumination, glimpses of unity, and the caterpillar, cocoon, and butterfly stages of spiritual unfoldment. "The Ten Virgins" of the Bible await the Divine. "The Prodigal Son" returns to the Father. Once home, in the full unitive state of consciousness, love turns its energy outward to embrace the world as one family, in the spirit of compassion and forgiveness. As we reflect on the stories of transformation, we see our own lives. We have been supported in our path in both large and small ways. What can we give as an expression of our gratitude to a world that has nourished us? It is not what we give, however, but the love we put into the giving. What can we give with as much compassion as possible? Have we been guided by the integrity and love within us? What would happen if we listen to the still, small voice within the silence of our heart? What would we need to change, to embrace, to trust?

In *Life at the Summit*, we discover that transformation reveals both our true nature and our humanity. "We are in the world but not of it," yet we experience the fullness of living our humanity. We chop wood, sweep the porch, prepare meals. But now work and play are one; outside is inside. In unity, self-interest has evaporated while compassion is revealed in heightened sensitivity for all that lives. A life of selfless giving, however, does not make us immune to normal human experiences. A physically ill Saint Teresa of Ávila, in one of her wagon pilgrimages to begin a dovecote of prayer, slept in a pig shed with no windows, under a blazing sun with bugs for company and unsolicited tambourine music playing in the background! She was also, however, wrapped in the eternal love, peace, and wisdom that is untouched by changing circumstances.

The stories of people who embody profound wisdom touch us because we sense the true nature of ourselves. The great sages and spiritual masters have charted a course to the Source of love and live in abiding union with it. They have discovered the way to be at peace in the midst of chaos; to live in profound trust and faith in the midst of criticism; to *be* forgiveness and acceptance in the midst of conflict.

Their stories inspire us to fulfill our own destiny, to live in the same spirit of harmony. As Gandhi said, "My life is my message." What does our life say? How can we touch our families, friends, communities with gentle compassion and wisdom? Where is the corner of our heart that we shelter jealousy or criticism? If we opened the protective door to compassion and forgiveness, how might our life be different? What change of heart would occur if we approached another in the spirit of the words, "Peace Be With You"?

Chapter I

The Ascent

The quest is spiritual mountaineering.

Paul Brunton

ॐॐॐॐॐॐॐ

The Sower and the Seed

A sower went out to sow his seed: and as he sowed, some fell by the way side; and it was trodden down, and the fowls of the air devoured it.

And some fell upon a rock; and as soon as it was sprung up, it withered away, because it lacked moisture.

And some fell among thorns; and the thorns sprang up with it, and choked it.

And other fell on good ground, and sprang up, and bare [bore] fruit an hundredfold. And when he had said these things, he cried, He that hath ears to hear, let him hear.

And his disciples asked him, saying, What might this parable be?

And he said. Unto you it is given to know the mysteries of the kingdom of God: but to others in parables; that seeing they might not see, and hearing they might not understand.

Now the parable is this: The seed is the word of God.

Those by the way side are they that hear; then cometh the devil, and taketh away the word out of their hearts, lest they should believe and be saved.

They on the rock *are they*, which, when they hear, receive the word with joy; and these have no root, which for a while believe, and in time of temptation fall away.

And that which fell among thorns are they, which, when they have heard, go forth, and are choked with cares and riches and pleasures of *this* life, and bring no fruit to perfection.

But that on the good ground are they, which in an honest and good heart, having heard the word, keep *it*, and bring forth fruit with patience.

The Gospel According to Saint Luke

What Do I Need to Know?

People were sitting around asking him questions. His answers were so beautiful. When the others had run out of questions, there was a long silence. Then I heard myself asking, "What do I need to know?"

He didn't answer. Just kept looking at me—for several minutes. Tears began to run down his cheek. But he looked happy enough.

Someone nudged me. "Ask him another question."

"No," he said. "That's the best question. I was thinking of the time I asked that very question of my master—when I first entered the monastery, fifty years ago. I will tell you how my master answered. He told me to take that question, 'what do I need to know?' and put it to every single monk. I did. Then he had me sit in solitude for a year, reflecting on their answers. Next he had me find a ship and sail around the world, putting my question to everyone I met. That took me six years. And I had to reflect on the answers in solitude for six years. That's how my master answered my question."

The room became silent again. "But Sir," I insisted, "please, what do *I* need to know?"

"Good," he answered. "I will give you—Christ, and that will be enough."

Father Theophane

The Dance

A disciple had asked permission to take part in the 'dance' of the Sufis.

The Sheikh said: 'Fast completely for three days. Then have luscious dishes cooked. If you then prefer the "dance," you may take part in it.'

Light

The true lover finds the light only if, like the candle, he is his own fuel, consuming himself.

Sufi

The frog does not drink up the pond in which he lives.

Indian Proverb

The soul that is attached to anything, however much good there may be in it, will not arrive at the liberty of divine union. For whether it be a strong wire rope or a slender and delicate thread that holds the bird, it matters not, if it really holds it fast; for, until the cord be broken, the bird cannot fly.

Saint John of the Cross

Just as, long ago, self consciousness appeared in the best specimens of our ancestral race in the prime of life, and gradually became more and more universal and appeared in the individual at an earlier and earlier age, until, as we see now, it has become almost universal and appears at the average of about three years—so will Cosmic Consciousness become more and more universal and appear earlier in the individual life until the race at large will possess this faculty. The same race and not the same; for a Cosmic Conscious race will not be the race which exists to-day, any more than the present race of men is the same race which existed prior to the evolution of self consciousness. The simple truth is, that there has lived on the earth, "appearing at intervals," for thousands of years among ordinary men, the first faint beginnings of another race; walking the earth and breathing the air with us, but at the same time walking another earth and breathing another air of which we know little or nothing, but which is, all the same, our spiritual life, as its absence would be our spiritual death. This new race is in act of being born from us, and in the near future it will occupy and possess the earth.

Richard Maurice Bucke, *Cosmic Consciousness*

Nature's purpose is neither food, nor drink, nor clothing, nor comfort, nor anything else from which God is left out. Whether you like it or not, whether you know it or not, secretly nature seeks and hunts and tries to ferret out the track in which God may be found.

Meister Eckhart

ह‍ाह‍ाह‍ाह‍ाह‍ाह‍ा

This fair lovely word "mother" is so sweet and so kind in itself that it cannot truly be said of anyone or to anyone except of him and to him who is the true Mother of life and of all things. To the property of motherhood belong nature, love, wisdom and knowledge, and this is God.

Julian of Norwich, Long Text of *Showings*

ह‍ाह‍ाह‍ाह‍ाह‍ाह‍ा

We lump together all things that are beyond the capacity of all of us collectively to understand—and one name we give to all those things together is God. Therefore, God is the creative force, the sustaining power, that which motivates toward constant change, the overall intelligence which governs the universe by physical and spiritual law, truth, love, goodness, kindness, beauty, the ever-present, all-pervading essence or spirit, which binds everything in the universe together and gives life to everything in the universe.

Peace Pilgrim

ह‍ाह‍ाह‍ाह‍ाह‍ाह‍ा

Our whole business in life is to restore to health the eye of the heart whereby God may be seen.

Saint Augustine

ह‍ाह‍ाह‍ाह‍ाह‍ाह‍ा

The man on this path, Arjuna, who resolves deep within himself to seek Me, attains singleness of purpose. For those who lack resolution the decisions are many-branched and endless.

Sri Krishna, *Bhagavad Gita*

We are speaking to souls that, in the end, enter the castle. These are very much absorbed in worldly affairs; but their desires are good; sometimes, though infrequently, they commend themselves to Our Lord; and they think about the state of their souls, though not very carefully. Full of a thousand preoccupations as they are, they pray only a few times a month, and as a rule they are thinking all the time of their preoccupations, for they are very much attached to them, and where their treasure is, there is their heart also. From time to time, however, they shake their minds free of them and it is a great thing that they should know themselves well enough to realize that they are not going the right way to reach the castle door. Eventually, they enter the first rooms on the lowest floor, but so many reptiles get in with them that they are unable to appreciate the beauty of the castle or to find peace within it. Still, they have done a good deal by entering at all.

Saint Teresa of Ávila

Nasrudin was now an old man looking back on his life. He sat with his friends in the tea shop telling his story.

"When I was young I was fiery—I wanted to awaken everyone. I prayed to Allah to give me the strength to change the world.

In mid-life I awoke one day and realized my life was half over and I had changed no one. So I prayed to Allah to give me the strength to change those close around me who so much needed it.

Alas, now I am old and my prayer is simpler. 'Allah,' I ask, 'please give me the strength to at least change myself.'"

Sufi

Q.   How is it possible to become selfless while leading a life of worldly activity?

A.   There is no conflict between work and wisdom.

Q.   Do you mean that one can continue all the old activities, in one's profession, for instance, and at the same time get enlightenment?

A.   Why not? But in that case one will not think that it is the old personality which is doing the work because one's consciousness will gradually become transformed until it enters in That which is beyond the little self.

Ramana Maharshi and the Path of Self-Knowledge

When I started out, my hair had started to turn to silver. My friends thought I was crazy. There was not one word of encouragement from them. They thought I would surely kill myself, walking all over. But that didn't bother me. I just went ahead and did what I had to do. They didn't know that with inner peace I felt plugged into the source of universal energy, which never runs out. There was much pressure to compromise my beliefs, but I would not be dissuaded. Lovingly, I informed my well-meaning friends of the existence of two widely divergent paths in life and of the free will within all to make their choice.

There is a well-worn road which is pleasing to the senses and gratifies worldly desires, but leads to nowhere. And there is the less traveled path, which requires purifications and relinquishments, but results in untold spiritual blessings.

Peace Pilgrim

"There is something that worries me a lot: I seem sometimes to hate everything and everybody. Hate them thoroughly and completely. Everyone seems to be irritating, ugly, even horrible. A constant irritation about practically everything surrounding me. I seem to have become barren and arid. Surely this is not an improvement?"

He smiled. "It is a stage one is passing. There was a time when I too hated everybody."

"But L. told me she feels universal love."

"This is something else. Once you love God, you love His Creation, and then you do not hate anymore."

Irina Tweedie

The will is inclined to love after seeing such countless signs of love; it would want to repay something; it especially keeps in mind how this true lover never leaves it; accompanying it and giving it life and being.

Then the intellect helps it to realize that it couldn't find a better friend, even if it were to live for many years.

Saint Teresa of Ávila

For where there is true love, a man is neither out of measure lifted up by prosperity, nor cast down by mishap; whether you give or take away from him, so long as he keeps his beloved, he has a spring of inward peace. Thus, even though thy outward man grieve, or weep downright, that may well be borne, if only thy inner man remain at peace, perfectly content with the will of God.

Johannes Tauler

Strength does not come from physical capacity. It comes from an indomitable will.

Mahatma Gandhi

The measure of your holiness is proportionate to the goodness of your will.

Jan van Ruysbroeck

To a Beggar With a Mite

Mother Teresa herself tells of the day she met a beggar who gave her everything he had. "Everybody gives you something," he said, "and I'm going to also—in fact, everything I have."

"That day," Mother Teresa says, "the beggar had received but one bolivar (a small coin). He gave it to me and said: 'Take it, Mother Teresa, for your poor.'"

Mother Teresa adds, "In my heart I felt that the poor man had given me more than the Nobel Prize because he gave me all he had. In all probability, no one gave him anything else that night and he went to bed hungry."

We have to be saints, not for the sake of being saints, but in order to offer Christ the opportunity to fully live in us. We have to be filled with love, faith, and purity, for the good of the poor whom we serve. Once we have learned how to look for God and his will, our contacts with the poor will serve to make saints of ourselves and others.

Mother Teresa

The glory of the Self is beheld by a few, and a few speak of its glory; a few hear about this glory, but there are many who listen without understanding.

Bhagavad Gita

২৪২৪২৪২৪২৪২৪

I noticed that my mind is only working in so far as my spiritual duties are concerned. For instance, I can write my diary; I remember fairly well all that he tells us; but I cannot do more than that; the brain is not good for anything else. And, what's more, nothing seems to matter any longer. Neither reading nor letter writing, nothing at all. All I want is to sit at his place, and even the silly, irritating chit-chat of the crowd around him seems to matter less and less. Everything seems to fall away from me as in a crazy dream when all the objects are crooked, vacillating and empty of content.

Irina Tweedie

২৪২৪২৪২৪২৪২৪

"What do you feel exactly?" he said suddenly, sharply, looking at me.

"Well, all the oceans and all the seas of the world seem to be concentrated in my head. Walking down the street I had just enough consciousness left to keep to the right side of the road and not to be run over by the traffic. Crossing the road I could not see where I was going. I thought it was dangerous. I could see only when I looked straight ahead; right and left seemed obliterated as in a mist.

"If I see an object, for instance this chair in front of me, between the image of the chair and the realization that it is a chair and not something else, there is an interval of a fraction of a second. I have to concentrate on each particular sensory object to be able to name it. Indeed Krishnamurti mentions in one of his works that we should abstain from naming the things around us so that the interval between seeing an object and naming it may become longer and longer and it may happen that one day, in that moment, illumination may come." He nodded.

"You spoke of a miracle a few days ago," he said slowly. "Have you still the courage to speak of miracles? The roar of all the oceans is in your head, or the mind is not there at all, or you don't sleep without being tired, while at my home your thinking process is slowed down so much that you 'sleep'; there is a peace not of this world in you which you cannot explain; or a longing so strong that life is not worth living; upheavals, premonitions; tell me, are these not miracles? Great and important miracles?"

His voice was soft and very gentle as if full of deep compassion. I lowered my eyes and felt small. Smaller than a grain of sand.

Irina Tweedie

Chapter II

Transformation of Consciousness

To the illumined man or woman, a clod of dirt, a stone, and gold are the same.

Sri Krishna, *Bhagavad Gita*

๛๛๛๛๛๛๛

The whole world was in absolute glory. There was such oneness with myself and the trees, the dirty children who throw stones, the mangy dogs and the fleas—all that was me. If I'd had any money, I would have given it all away . . . .

Irina Tweedie

๛๛๛๛๛๛๛

I was sitting on a low wall on the outskirts of the town of Chittagong. Across the road was a wayside teashop stall, with the proprietor in full view serving two customers. The branches of two small trees next to the stall waved in the moderately strong breeze and the sun shone with some glare on the

167

white dusty road, along which came some fishermen with baskets of fish on their heads. From the second storey of a nearby building I could hear a nautch tune. Then, as the fishermen came abreast of me, one fish still alive, flapped up and seemed to stand on its tail and bow. I felt great compassion for the fish.

Suddenly everything was transformed, transfigured, translated, transcended. All was fused into one. I was the fish. The sun sang and the road sang. The music shone. The hands of the stall-keeper danced. All in time with the same music. They were the music and I was the music and I was the fish, the fishermen, the hands of the stall-keeper, the trees, the branches, the road, the sun, the music; all one and nothing separate. Not parts of the one but the one itself.

Meg Maxwell and Verena Tschudin, *Seeing the Invisible*
from The Alister Hardy Research Center

ﻌﻌﻌﻌﻌﻌﻌﻌ

All that is sweet, delightful, and amiable in this world, in the serenity of the air, the fineness of seasons, the joy of light, the melody of sounds, the beauty of colours, the fragrancy of smells, the splendour of precious stones, is nothing else but Heaven breaking through the veil of this world, manifesting itself in such a degree and darting forth in such variety so much of its own nature.

William Law

ﻌﻌﻌﻌﻌﻌﻌﻌ

The second of these experiences came about seven years after the first one, when I visited a meditation retreat center in Southern California with a group of friends with whom there had been several days of deep sharing and communication. As we sat in that room at the top of the mountain, a room which had been set aside for prayer and meditation and which was visited by people from all over the world, I found myself enfolded in the most transcending silence I had ever known. This silence fell on me like a holy cloak and wrapped me into such a shelter of love that tears flowed silently from the recesses of some untouched depth. Weeping is not something I do a lot, but when tears come I have discovered they often carry healing, sometimes for myself, sometimes for others. I wept that day because of the sense of the tremendous Love that seemed to be everywhere. Never a word was uttered by any of us during the half hour we were in that room, but each second was a profound experience of Love in the highest dimension.

I concluded later that others in that room with me were important agents in releasing the higher vibrations of consciousness, and that the atmosphere of the room itself may have been previously purified by the holier thoughts of those who visited it. I am sure that more than just mortals were there. I do believe that He stood in our midst, just as He promised He would when two or three gathered in His name. His manifestation in the gathered group will always have a dimension that we cannot find in solitude.

When we left that mountain and drove back through the town, I had a visible apprehension of life that was new. It was a bright, sunny day; yet some people on the streets seemed to be standing under shadows, while others looked radiant with a glow of inner light. I seemed to have been granted the privilege for a few minutes of seeing the inner expression of people, rather than the outer, and could understand then how we all dwell in varying shades of light or darkness according to our own spiritual awareness. That apprehension has not returned to me since that day, and I do not think it need return. It was given to me once and for once only to make me perceptive to the fact that the reality of a person is not in the physical or outer appearance. Since the physical is all we normally see, we must be very cautious with our judgments because we lack full information. Jesus said that we may judge by righteous judgments only, and I understand now what He meant: Not until we have looked on the inner reality of a person do we dare make any assessments. Yet the marvel was that for those people standing that day in shadows, I felt not the slightest judgment but rather an outgoing compassion.

I call that experience my personal Mount of Transfiguration when, with Jesus and a few of His twentieth century disciples, I entered briefly into the higher realms of the Christ Consciousness and summarily explored a universe wider than my own views of it had been before.

The final experience in this land of expanded consciousness that I want to share came in the summer of 1975 when Beverly and I, with a company of twenty-eight friends from our church, went down the Colorado River of the Grand Canyon from Lee's Ferry, Arizona, to Lake Mead, Nevada (a distance of nearly three hundred miles), on motor-powered rafts. It took us eight days and this particular experience happened to me on the third night. I share it with some trepidation, for it is so mysterious that I am not sure I fully understand it, nor do I know why it occurred when it did. It came about in this way.

The sun was low on canyon walls when we pulled our boats from the heavy current of the river onto a sandy spit that extended itself to meet us. It had been a heady day of following the river, moving serenely for long stretches at a time, and then periodically erupting with it in a foment of churning rapids that required all the skill of the boatmen to keep us from turning over. It had been an exciting day and a good day, but now the prospect of some dry clothes, a hot meal, and a night's sleep seemed even more appealing.

We cooked our meal over the open fire, ate it sitting on rocks that were partly buried in clean white sand, and for the thousandth time we gazed toward the top of the sculptured walls of the canyon that soared thousands of feet above us. Words were few, and when they came, were spoken in quiet, reverential tones as though we were in some great cathedral.

Darkness came quickly, and we made our way to the places we had selected to sleep. Beverly and I chose a little promontory close to the river, scooped out some hollows in the sand to fit the contours of our bodies, spread our sleeping bags, and stretched out. For a few moments I tried in vain to imagine what life was like back home in the midst of a city, but it was too far away and too unreal. I contemplated anxiously the fact that there were engineers and technicians who wanted to destroy this place of natural wonder by damming the river for a power source, and I vowed not to sit idly by and let that happen. We prayed together briefly, and in a short time I fell asleep.

I must have slept for a few hours when suddenly I awoke. The full moon, just touching the edge of the canyon walls, was transforming my cavern of darkness into a place of ethereal mystery and intoxicating loveliness. All the usual things around me were starting to change in that miraculous new light. The mounded shapes of my companions in their sleeping bags a few feet away emerged from the gentle blur of darkness into distinct forms as the moon began to touch them.

Suddenly I saw in those early moments of waking, beyond any words of mine to describe, how wildly beautiful and joyously wonderful is all of life. I felt myself drawn into the luminosity of the firmament until it was as though I was the link that united the heavens to the earth. Hanging breathless and suspended in space and time, I felt an irresistible and tremendous sense of Love take possession of me, the same flooding joyousness that I had experienced that day at the ocean and again on the mountaintop, except that this time it seemed even more intense.

For those glorified moments I was in love with every living thing. No, it was more than that—I *was* every living thing. I was the water rushing in its headlong course towards the sea. I was the tamarisk and willow trees bending in the gentle night breeze. I was the invisible creature scurrying in the grass at the edge of my sand hollow. I was the little bat patterning the space over my head. I was my friends sleeping nearby. I was the luminous moon and each apex of the sparkling triangle of stars. I was all of it, and I was madly in love with all of it.

Then, as if the miracle of that moment were not enough, I heard a faint metallic humming like the sigh of electric wires, which broke into gentle crescendos of sound. It seemed as though every chord and note of music I could imagine was being sounded at once, yet in perfect harmony and attunement. Of myself I was no longer conscious. My very soul flowed out of me into the abundance and reality of Life and into the deep, ecstatic joy of all living things.

I cannot say how long it lasted, perhaps not more than ten minutes, but even as it faded, I was left with a wholly exquisite feeling. There was none of the usual burden of responsibility I often felt, and life spread out before me as a glorious, shining happiness.

I suppose it could be labeled a mystical experience, but no title and no description can do it justice. I only know that for a brief space of transcended time, while lying on the bank of the Colorado River in the heart of the Grand Canyon on a warm August night, I touched the hand of God as He joined me and all other grains of sand to the stars and moon, and that for one full intoxicating instant I stood on the edge of eternity where, accompanied by the music of the spheres, I glimpsed the face of the universe.

Rodney R. Romney

Imagine if all the tumult of the body were to quiet down, along with all our busy thoughts . . . . Imagine if all things that are perishable grew still . . . . And imagine if that moment were to go on and on, leaving behind all other sights and sounds but this one vision which ravishes and absorbs and fixes the beholder in joy; so that the rest of eternal life were like that moment of illumination which leaves us breathless.

Saint Augustine

I was at work, busy on my job, when suddenly this sensation of peace and compassion 'descended' around me, accompanied by the feeling of glorious *beauty*, as if all the beauty in the world would only be one tiny fraction of this beauty. It only lasted a few minutes. There was nothing to see, hear, touch, taste, or smell.

The experience was strongly reminiscent of a passage in the *Mandukya Upanishad:*

like two birds of golden plumage, inseparable
companions, the individual self and the immortal self
are perched on the same tree. The former tastes of the
sweet and bitter fruits of the tree; the latter, tasting of
neither, calmly observes.

Meg Maxwell and Verena Tschudin, *Seeing the Invisible*
from The Alister Hardy Research Center

When I undertake to tell the best, I find I cannot.
My tongue is ineffectual on its pivots,
My breath will not be obedient to its organs,
I become a dumb man.

Walt Whitman

The person in the peak experience usually feels himself to be at the peak of his powers . . . . He feels more intelligent, more perceptive, wittier, stronger, or more graceful than at other times. He is at concert pitch, at the top of his form. This is not only felt subjectively but can be seen by the observer.

Abraham Maslow

❧❧❧❧❧❧❧❧

'Poor boy, the mountains couldn't give you what you wanted.' Master spoke caressingly, comfortingly. His calm gaze was unfathomable. 'Your heart's desire shall be fulfilled.'

Sri Yukteswar seldom indulged in riddles; I was bewildered. He struck gently on my chest above the heart. My body became immovably rooted; breath was drawn out of my lungs as if by some huge magnet. Soul and mind instantly lost their physical bondage and streamed out like a fluid piercing light from my every pore. The flesh was as though dead, yet in my intense awareness I knew that never before had I been fully alive. My sense of identity was no longer narrowly confined to a body, but embraced the circumambient atoms. People on distant streets seemed to be moving gently over my own remote periphery. The roots of plants and trees appeared through a dim transparency of the soil; I discerned the inward flow of their sap.

The whole vicinity lay bare before me. My ordinary frontal vision was now changed to a vast spherical sight, simultaneously all-perceptive. Through the back of my head I saw men strolling down Rai Ghat Lane, and noticed also a white cow who was leisurely approaching. When she reached the space in front of the open ashram gate, I observed her as though with my physical eyes. As she passed by, behind the brick wall I saw her clearly still.

All objects within my panoramic gaze trembled and vibrated like quick motion pictures. My body, Master's, the pillared courtyard, the furniture and floor, the trees and sunshine, occasionally became violently agitated, until all melted into a luminescent sea; even as sugar crystals, thrown into a glass of water, dissolve after being shaken. The unifying light alternated with materializations of form, the metamorphoses revealing the law of cause and effect in creation.

An oceanic joy broke upon calm endless shores of my soul. The Spirit of God, I realized, is exhaustless bliss; His body is countless tissues of light. A swelling glory within me began to envelop towns, continents, the earth, solar and stellar systems, tenuous nebulae, and floating universes. The entire cosmos, gently luminous, like a city seen afar at night, glimmered within the infinitude of my being. The dazzling light beyond the sharply etched global outlines faded somewhat at the farthest edges; there I could see a mellow radiance, ever-undiminished. It was indescribably subtle; the planetary pictures were formed of a grosser light.

The divine dispersion of rays poured from an eternal source, blazing into galaxies, transfigured with ineffable auras. Again and again, I saw the creative beams condense into constellations, then resolve into sheets of transparent flame . . .

Suddenly the breath returned to my lungs. With a disappointment almost unbearable, I realized that my infinite immensity was lost. Once more I was limited to the humiliating cage of a body, not easily accommodative to the Spirit. Like a prodigal child, I had run away from my macrocosmic home and imprisoned myself in a paltry microcosm.

Paramahansa Yogananda, *Autobiography of a Yogi*

❧❧❧❧❧❧❧❧❧

'Sitting one day in his room, his eyes fell upon a burnished pewter dish, which reflected the sunshine with such marvellous splendour that he fell into an inward ecstasy, and it seemed to him as if he could now look into the principles and deepest foundations of things. He believed that it was only a fancy, and in order to banish it from his mind he went out upon the green. But here he remarked that he gazed into the very heart of things, the very herbs and grass, and that actual nature harmonized with what he had inwardly seen. He said nothing of this to anyone, but praised and thanked God in silence.'

The Varieties of Religious Experience

❧❧❧❧❧❧❧❧❧

It was a kind of waking trance which I have frequently had, quite up from boyhood, when I have been all alone. This has generally come upon me through repeating my own name two or three times to myself silently, till all at once, as it were out of the intensity of the consciousness of individuality, the individuality itself seemed to dissolve and fade away into boundless being, and this not a confused state, but the clearest of the clearest, the surest of the surest, the weirdest of the weirdest, utterly beyond words where death was an almost laughable impossibility, the loss of personality (if so it were) being no extinction but the only true life . . . . This might be the state which St. Paul describes. Whether in the body I cannot tell or whether out of the body I cannot tell.

Alfred Tennyson, *Memoir*

❧❧❧❧❧❧❧❧❧

. . . it was as if something snapped inside my head, and the whole of me was streaming out ceaselessly, without diminishing, on and on. There was no "me"—just flowing. Just being. A feeling of unending expansion, just streaming forth . . . . But all this I know only later, when I tried to remember it. When I first came back the first clear, physical sensation was of intense cold.

It was shattering. But what was it? Was it prayer? Not in the ordinary sense. For a prayer there must be somebody to pray. But I was not. I did not exist.

The door was open; the door to what? Whatever it was, it was wonderful. There must be an infinite sea of it. Like a terrific pull of one's whole being. Is this the "prayer of the heart"; is this "merging"? I don't know. Because when I am in it, there is no mind. I seem not to exist at all; and when the mind begins to know something about it, it is already past. But even the idea of praying to somebody or something seems pointless now . . . .

. . . This is ABSOLUTE security, I said to myself. But to reach it, one has to traverse the no-man's land; one has to wade through the morass of insecurity, where there is no foothold of any kind and where one cannot even see the ground under one's feet . . . .

And with a sigh of relief, I fell asleep, blown out suddenly, like a candle by a gust of wind.

Irina Tweedie

ᘓᘉᘓᘉᘓᘉᘓᘉᘓᘉᘓᘉ

'In the twenty-fifth year of his age, he was again surrounded by the divine light and replenished with the heavenly knowledge; insomuch as going abroad in the fields to a green before Neys Gate, at Goerlitz, he there sat down and, viewing the herbs and grass of the field in his inward light, he saw into their essences, use and properties, which were discovered to him by their lineaments, figures and signatures. In like manner he beheld the whole creation, and from that foundation he afterwards wrote his book, *De signature Rerum*. In the unfolding of those mysteries before his understanding he had a great measure of joy, yet returned home and took care of his family and lived in great peace and silence, scarce intimating to any these wonderful things that had befallen him, and in the year 1610, being again taken into this light, lest the mysteries revealed to him should pass through him as a stream, and rather for a memorial than intending any publication, he wrote his first book, called *Aurora,* or the *Morning Redness.*'

The Varieties of Religious Experience

ᘓᘉᘓᘉᘓᘉᘓᘉᘓᘉᘓᘉ

For you the world outside will now stand transformed as the very expression or manifestation of God—everywhere the Light of God will dazzle your eyes; even in the apparent diversity and activity of nature you will strangely be conscious of an all-pervading stillness and peace of the Eternal—a consciousness which is unshakably permanent. You will also feel that you are liberated from the harassing dualities of life followed by the crowning experience of an abiding state of ineffable ecstasy.

Swami Ramdas

ᘓᘉᘓᘉᘓᘉᘓᘉᘓᘉᘓᘉ

At times it certainly seemed to me as if I were looking at a painting, but on many other occasions it appeared to be no painting but Christ Himself, such was the clarity with which He was pleased to appear to me. Yet there were times when the vision was so indistinct that I did think it was a painting, though it bore no resemblance even to the most perfect of earthly pictures, and I have seen some good ones. No, it would be absurd to speak of any resemblance; the vision was no more like a painting than a portrait is like a living man. However well a portrait is painted, it can never look completely natural, for it is plainly a dead thing.

The Life of Saint Teresa

☙☙☙☙☙

It was in the early spring, at the beginning of his thirty-sixth year. He and two friends had spent the evening reading Wordsworth, Shelley, Keats, Browning, and especially Whitman. They parted at midnight and he had a long drive in a hansom (it was an English city). His mind, deeply under the influence of the ideas, images and emotions called up by the reading and talk of the evening, was calm and peaceful. He was in a state of quiet, almost passive enjoyment. All at once, without warning of any kind, he found himself wrapped around as it were by a flame-coloured cloud. For an instant he thought of fire, some sudden conflagration in the great city; the next he knew the light was in himself. Directly afterwards came upon him a sense of exultation, of immense joyousness accompanied or immediately followed by an intellectual illumination quite impossible to describe. Into his brain streamed one momentary lightning-flash of the Brahmic splendour which has ever since lightened his life; upon his heart fell one drop of Brahmic bliss, leaving thenceforward for always an aftertaste of heaven. Among other things . . . he saw and knew that the cosmos is not dead matter but a living Presence, that the soul of man is immortal, that the universe is so built and ordered that without peradventure all things work together for the good of each and all, that the foundation principle of the world is what we call love and that the happiness of everyone in the long run is absolutely certain. He claims he learned more within the few seconds during which the illumination lasted than in previous months or even years of study and that he learned much that no study could ever have taught.

Richard Maurice Bucke, *Cosmic Consciousness*

☙☙☙☙☙

Just as a reservoir is of little use to people when the country is flooded all around, so the scriptures are of little use to the illumined man who sees the Lord everywhere.

Bhagavad Gita

☙☙☙☙☙

There were hills and valleys, lots of hills and valleys, in that spiritual growing up period. Then in the midst of the struggle there came a wonderful mountaintop experience—the first glimpse of what the life of inner peace was like.

That came when I was out walking in the early morning. All of a sudden I felt very uplifted, more uplifted than I had ever been. I remember I knew *timelessness* and *spacelessness* and *lightness.* I did not seem to be walking on the earth. There were no people or even animals around, but every flower, every bush, every tree seemed to wear a halo. There was a light emanation around everything and flecks of gold fell like slanted rain through the air. This experience is sometimes called the illumination period.

The most important part of it was not the phenomena: the important part of it was the realization of the oneness of all creation. Not only all human beings—I knew before that all human beings are one. But now I knew also a oneness with the rest of creation. The creatures that walk the earth and the growing things of the earth. The air, the water, the earth itself. And, most wonderful of all, *a oneness with that which permeates all and binds all together and gives life to all.* A oneness with that which many would call God.

Peace Pilgrim

I said to him, "Our relationship to God is something entirely different from what we usually imagine it to be. We think that the relationship of God and Man is a duality. But it is not so. I have found that our relationship to God is something quite different. It is a merging, without words, without thought even; into 'something.' Something so tremendous, so endless, merging in Infinite Love, physical body and all, disappearing in it. And the physical body is under suffering; it is taut like a spring in this process of annihilation. This is our experience of God and it cannot be otherwise."

"What you have said is absolutely correct," he nodded gravely.

Irina Tweedie

When I ended my first cross-country walk I felt so thankful that I had not failed to do what I had been called to do. I either said or thought to myself, "Isn't it wonderful that God can do something through me!"

Afterward I slept at the Grand Central Station railroad terminal in New York City.

When I came into the state between sleep and wakefulness, I had an impression that an indescribably beautiful voice was speaking words of encouragement: *"You are my beloved daughter in whom I am well pleased."* When I came into full wakefulness it seemed as though a celestial orchestra had just finished playing in the station, with its echoes still lingering on. I walked out into the cold morning, but I felt warm. I walked along the cement sidewalk, but I felt I was walking on clouds. The feeling of living in harmony with divine purpose has never left me.

Peace Pilgrim

He showed her a most beautiful crystal globe, made in the shape of a castle, and containing seven mansions, in the seventh and innermost of which was the King of Glory, in the greatest splendour, illumining and beautifying them all. The nearer one got to the centre, the stronger was the light; outside the palace limits everything was foul, dark and infected with toads, vipers and other venomous creatures.

While she was wondering at this beauty, which by God's grace can dwell in the human soul, the light suddenly vanished. Although the King of Glory did not leave the mansions, the crystal globe was plunged into darkness, became as black as coal and emitted an insufferable odor, and the venomous creatures outside the palace boundaries were permitted to enter the castle.

Saint Teresa of Ávila

How sweet it is to love, and to be dissolved, and as it were to bathe myself in thy love.

Thomas à Kempis

Swiftly arose and spread around me the peace and joy and
knowledge that pass all the art and argument of the earth;
And I know that the hand of God is the elderhand of my
    own,
And I know that the spirit of God is the eldest brother of my
    own,
And that all the men ever born are also my brothers . . . and
the women my sisters and lovers.

Walt Whitman, *Song of Myself*

Why, who makes much of a miracle?
As for me I know of nothing else but miracles.
Whether I walk the streets of Manhattan,
Or dart my sight over the roofs of houses toward the sky,
Or wade with naked feet along the beach just in the edge of
    the water,
Or stand under trees in the woods . . . .
Or look at strangers opposite me riding in the car,
Or watch honey-bees busy around the hive . . . .
Or the exquisite delicate thin curve of the new moon in
    spring—

These with the rest, one and all, are to me miracles . . . .

The smallest sprout shows there is really no death.
And if there was, it led forward life . . . .
All goes onward and outward, nothing collapses.

Walt Whitman

Sri Krishna: The Illumined Man

He lives in wisdom who sees himself in all and all in him, whose love for the Lord of Love has consumed every selfish desire and sense craving tormenting the heart.

Not agitated by greed, nor hankering after pleasure, he lives free from lust and fear and anger.

Fettered no more by selfish attachments, he is not elated by good fortune nor depressed by bad. Such is the seer.

Even as a tortoise draws in its limbs, the sage can draw in his senses at will. But he lives in wisdom who subdues them and keeps his mind ever absorbed in Me.

When you keep thinking about sense objects, attachment comes. Attachment breeds desire, the lust of possession which, when thwarted, burns to anger. Anger clouds the judgment and robs you of the power to learn from past mistakes. Lost is the discriminative faculty, and your life is utter waste.

Aspirants abstain from sense pleasures, but they still crave for them. These cravings all disappear when they see the highest goal. Even of those who tread the path, the stormy senses can sweep off the mind.

Bhagavad Gita

Watching the sun rise I sat for a while outside. This love. My God, what love! All the beauties of this wonderful nature around are very secondary, are just on the edge of consciousness; but deep, deep within there is this love and this is the ONLY REALITY—this love that digs deep into the heart its blazing abyss, this love that enwraps and exalts my whole being and the whole of creation as one. We are one, how very true; if only we could realize it, everything would be so very different. If only . . . . But how steep is the path that leads to this realization to this supreme experience. We have to be emptied, made nothing, to be filled with thy divine love, with the purity of thy love, O God! Guruji, now I understand; I was emptied to be filled; I was made naught to be *human*. A steam-roller went over me and I was the better for it; but what managed to get up afterward was something very different from the human being who faced you in 1961!

And in bed I was thinking that it does not matter if I stay with closed eyes or go outside to watch the sunrise . . . . It is all in me . . . not outside me. I can be in a cave, in a prison, in eternal darkness, and it would matter little, if I had this glory within forever . . . .

Was reflecting that this feeling of divinity has no pride in it; it is on the contrary a very humble feeling. It is: I am nothing before Thee.

Irina Tweedie

The true impulses are very different. We do not pile the wood beneath the fire ourselves; it is rather as if it were already burning and we were suddenly thrown in to be consumed. The soul makes no effort to feel the pain caused it by the Lord's presence, but is pierced to the depths of its entrails, or sometimes to the heart, by an arrow, so that it does not know what is wrong or what it desires. It knows quite well that it desires God and that the arrow seems to have been tipped with some poison which makes it so hate itself out of love of the Lord that it is willing to give up its life for Him. It is impossible to describe or explain the way in which God wounds the soul, or the very great pain He inflicts on it, so that it hardly knows what it is doing. But this is so sweet a pain that no delight in the whole world can be more pleasing. The soul, as I have said, would be glad always to be dying of this ill.

This combination of joy and sorrow so bewildered me that I could not understand how such a thing could be. O what it is to see a soul wounded! I mean one that sufficiently understands its condition as to be able to call itself wounded, and for so excellent a cause. It clearly sees that this love has come to it through no action of its own, but that out of the very great love that the Lord has for it a spark seems suddenly to have fallen on it and set it all on fire. O how often, when I am in this state, do I remember that verse of David, *As the heart panteth after the water brooks,* which I seem to see literally fulfilled in myself.

The Life of Saint Teresa of Ávila

And from that time that it was shewed I desired oftentimes to learn what was our Lord's meaning. And fifteen years after, and more, I was answered in ghostly understanding, saying thus: 'Wouldst thou learn our Lord's meaning in this thing? Learn it well: love was his meaning. Who shewed it thee? Love. What shewed he thee? Love. Wherefore shewed it he? For love. Hold thee therein and thou shalt learn and know more in the same. But thou shalt never know nor learn therein other thing without end.' Thus was I learned that love was our Lord's meaning.

Julian of Norwich, *Revelations of Divine Love*

God is Love

God is love, and he who abides in love abides in God, and God abides in him.

Christianity

He that loveth not, knoweth not God. For God is love.

Buddhism

Love is the beginning and end of the Torah.

Judaism

Love belongs to the high nobility of Heaven, and is the quiet home where man should dwell.

Confucianism

Sane and insane, all are searching lovelorn
For Him, in mosque, temple, church, alike.
For only God is the One God of Love,
And Love calls from all these, each one Him home.

Sufism

And so it came . . . it slipped itself into my heart, silently, imperceptibly, and I looked at it with wonder. It was still, small; a light-blue flame trembling softly, and it had the infinite sweetness of first love, like an offering of fragrant flowers made with gentle hands, the heart full of stillness and wonder and peace.

"Love will be produced," you [Guruji] said. And since then I kept wondering how it will come to me. Will it be like the voice from the Burning Bush, the Voice of God as Moses heard it? Will it be like a flash of lightning out of a blue sky making the world about me a blaze of glory? Or will it be, as I suggested, that you will produce Love in general, Love of everything, and the Teacher will be included in it? But I told [her] that it could not be so for me; to be able to surrender completely, to sweep away all resistance, it must be big, tremendous, complete; without reserve; without limit; the conditionless, absolute forgetting oneself.

But what I felt was not so. It was just a tender longing, so gentle, so full of infinite sweetness.

Like all laws governing this universe, love will follow the way of least resistance. In all my life I never knew the feeling of love flashing suddenly into my heart. It always came softly, timidly, like a small flower at the side of the road, so easily crushed by the boots of those who may pass by; growing slowly, steadily, increasing until it became vast, sweeping like a tidal wave, engulfing everything that stood in its way and at last filling all my life. So it was in the past and this time too; it is coming to me in the same way. I suppose because our hearts are made in a certain way we cannot help being what we are.

Irina Tweedie

ช่ะช่ะช่ะช่ะ

This prayer, then, is a little spark of the Lord's true love which He begins to enkindle in the soul; and He desires that the soul grow in the understanding of what this love accompanied by delight is. For anyone who has experience, it is impossible not to understand soon that this little spark cannot be acquired. Yet, this nature of ours is so eager for delights that it tries everything; but it is quickly left cold because however much it may desire to light the fire and obtain this delight, it doesn't seem to be doing anything else than throwing water on it and killing it.

Saint Teresa of Ávila

ช่ะช่ะช่ะช่ะ

Undisciplined love dwells in the senses for it is still entangled with earthly things . . . . Disciplined love lives in the soul and rises above the human senses and forbids the body its own will. It is modest and very still. It folds its wings and listens to an unspeakable voice and gazes into incomprehensible light and seeks eagerly the will of its Lord.

Mechthild of Magdeburg

When God sees the Soul pure as it was in its origins,
He tugs at it with a glance,
draws it and binds it to Himself with a fiery love
that by itself could annihilate the immortal soul.
In so acting, God so transforms the soul in Him
that it knows nothing other than God;
and He continues to draw it up into His fiery love
until He restores it
to that pure state from which it first issued.
These rays purify and then annihilate.
The soul becomes like gold
that becomes purer as it is fired,
all dross being cast out.

Having come to the point of twenty-four carats,
gold cannot be purified any further;
and this is what happens to the soul
in the fire of God's love.

Saint Catherine of Genoa, *Purgation and Purgatory*

A deer that has eaten a snake rushes to water in order to neutralize the poison; but a soul wounded by the arrows of God drinks deep draughts of ceaseless longing for her assailant.

Philokalia 3:50

As iron put into the fire loseth its rust and becometh clearly red-hot, so he that wholly turneth himself unto God puts off all slothfulness, and is transformed into a new man.

Thomas à Kempis

When going to Pushpa's for lunch today, I was so acutely aware of the suffering of nature, of so many little things dying in the drought. The air boiling, the soil parched, Guruji's garden withered, leaves hanging from the branches, getting brittle and yellow.

Still, I was aware of a leaden peace; joyless, dark, but nonetheless, peace. There was much heartache, a permanent feature nowadays. Even the feeling of love is no more. Such is the maya. Nothing remains save the pain in the heart.

Irina Tweedie

No life can express, nor tongue so much as name, what this enflaming, all-consuming love of God is. It is brighter than the sun, it is sweeter than anything called sweet; it is stronger than all strength; it is more nutrimental than food, more cheering to the heart than wine, and more pleasant than all the joy and pleasantness of the world. Whoever obtaineth it is richer than any monarch on earth; and he who getteth it is nobler than any emperor can be, and more potent and absolute than all power and authority.

Jacob Boehme

The Prodigal Son

And he said, A certain man had two sons:

And the younger of them said to *his* father, Father, give me the portion of goods that falleth *to me*. And he divided unto them *his* living.

And not many days after the younger son gathered all together, and took his journey into a far country, and there wasted his substance with riotous living.

And when he had spent all, there arose a mighty famine in that land; and he began to be in want.

And he went and joined himself to a citizen of that country; and he sent him into his fields to feed swine.

And he would fain have filled his belly with the husks that the swine did eat: and no man gave unto him.

And when he came to himself, he said, How many hired servants of my father's have bread enough and to spare, and I perish with hunger!

I will arise and go to my father, and will say unto him, Father, I have sinned against heaven, and before thee,

And am no more worthy to be called thy son: make me as one of thy hired servants.

And he arose, and came to his father. But when he was yet a great way off, his father saw him, and had compassion, and ran, and fell on his neck, and kissed him.

And the son said unto him, Father, I have sinned against heaven, and in thy sight, and am no more worthy to be called thy son.

But the father said to his servants, Bring forth the best robe, and put *it* on him; and put a ring on his hand, and shoes on *his* feet:

And bring hither the fatted calf, and kill *it;* and let us eat, and be merry:

For this my son was dead, and is alive again; he was lost, and is found. And they began to be merry.

Now his elder son was in the field: and as he came and drew nigh to the house, he heard musick and dancing.

And he called one of the servants, and asked what these things meant.

And he said unto him, Thy brother is come; and thy father hath killed the fatted calf, because he hath received him safe and sound.

And he was angry, and would not go in: therefore came his father out, and intreated him.

And he answering said to *his* father, Lo, these many years do I serve thee, neither transgressed I at any time thy commandment: and yet thou never gavest me a kid, that I might make merry with my friends:

But as soon as this thy son was come, which hath devoured thy living with harlots, thou hast killed for him the fatted calf.

And he said unto him, Son, thou art ever with me, and all that I have is thine.

It was meet that we should make merry, and be glad: for this thy brother was dead, and is alive again; and was lost, and is found.

Gospel According to Saint Luke

I had been reading in the garden when I felt an invisible film, or thin veil, come down over my head, and shroud my mind . . . . Swiftly and decisively, all had been done in silence; yet, however simple and innocent its quiet descent, this act was, in effect, terrible and awful—the Almighty had simply lowered the boom.

The first thing I noticed was that I could no longer see the words on the page; suddenly, they had become characters without meaning. It was several days before I could read again, and then it was totally without meaning. For years afterward, I could only derive meaning when and where God permitted some understanding to break through; these breakthroughs would shed light on the mystery of God's ways in my soul, in creation, or in his great plan for man . . . . Apart from the practical knowledge necessary for daily living (horse sense), my mind was plunged into darkness, wherein the only way of knowing was by this special light; I had to trust in it implicitly, because there was no other way of seeing.

. . . Although the mind is now left in a painful, empty void, this symptom is actually the lesser of two that mark this phase of the dark night. If it is dark and empty "above" (in the mind), so too, it is dark and empty "below" (in our interior). After the descent of the veil, I looked inward to encounter not the usual, obscure presence of God, but a gaping black hole where He had been and on seeing this, there arose from this center a pain so terrible, so enormous, that I wondered how it could be contained. It was the feeling of being cauterized, branded by God in the depths of my being—depths I never knew I had till then. The pain was beyond control, verging on the limits of human endurance with no escape or cooperation possible; in a word, the pain was all! For the next nine months, this pain came and went as it pleased, in daily bouts, several times a day. My understanding was that God had some merciless work to do here, and would not relent until His mysterious job was done . . . .

Eventually, I learned that the best protection against this pain was to fully accept it, and that by virtually sinking into it, sinking into my feeling of utter misery and nothingness, the pain lost much of its punch. It seems that a deep submissiveness is essential here, because, with the increasing ability to hold still, let go, sink in, and thereby come to naught, the pain subsides, and eventually disappears. After this came peace of soul, though it was initially loveless and joyless, it was nevertheless, as painless and restful as the calm after a great storm. Then, from out of this nothingness, this ash-heap of misery, there gradually emerged a whole new life.

Bernadette Roberts

ε▲ε▲ε▲ε▲ε▲ε▲ε▲

A ray of sunlight shining upon a smudgy window is unable to illumine that window completely and transform it into its own light. It could do this if the window were cleaned and polished. The less the film and stain are wiped away, the less the window will be illumined; and the cleaner the window is, the brighter will be its illumination. The extent of illumination is not dependent upon the ray of sunlight but upon the window. If the window is totally clean and pure, the sunlight will so transform and illumine it that to all appearances the window will be identical with the ray of sunlight and shine just as the sun's ray. Although obviously the nature of the window is distinct from that of the sun's ray (even if the two seem identical), we can assert that the window is the ray or light of the sun by participation.

The soul upon which the divine light of God's being is ever shining, or better, in which it is always dwelling by nature is like this window, as we have affirmed.

Saint John of the Cross

ε▲ε▲ε▲ε▲ε▲ε▲ε▲

The male God Katai-Jin, who descended into Your body on November 27 last year, and the Female God Amaterau Meokami who descended on August 11, have united as one God, making your body a temple, and thus forming the "Trinity"!

Kitamura Sayo (O-gami-sama)

૨**ર્ટ્રે**ર્ટ્રેટ્રેટ્રેટ્રેટ્રે

Love consists not in feeling great things but in having great detachment and in suffering for the Beloved.

Saint John of the Cross

૨**ર્ટ્રે**ર્ટ્રેટ્રેટ્રેટ્રેટ્રે

Seek refuge in the attitude of detachment and you will amass the wealth of spiritual awareness. The man who is motivated only by desire for the fruits of his action, and anxious about the results, is miserable indeed.

Bhagavad Gita

૨**ર્ટ્રે**ર્ટ્રેટ્રેટ્રેટ્રેટ્રે

The spiritual sleep which the soul has in the bosom of its Beloved comprises enjoyment of all the calm and rest and quiet of the peaceful night, and it receives God together with this, a dark and profound Divine intelligence, and for this reason the Bride says that her Beloved is to her the tranquil night.

Saint John of the Cross, *Spiritual Canticle*

૨**ર્ટ્રે**ર્ટ્રેટ્રેટ્રેટ્રેટ્રે

I imagine I was born in a country which is covered in thick fog. I never had the experience of contemplating the joyful appearance of nature flooded and transformed by the brilliance of the sun. It is true that from childhood I have heard people speak of these marvels, and I know the country in which I am living is not really my true fatherland.

Saint Thérèse of Lisieux, *Story of a Soul*

૨**ર્ટ્રે**ર્ટ્રેટ્રેટ્રેટ્રેટ્રે

And now I said, let me show in a figure how far our nature is enlightened or unenlightened: Behold! human beings living in an underground cave, which has a mouth open towards the light and reaching all along the cave; here they have been from their childhood, and have their legs and necks chained so that they cannot move, and can only see before them, being prevented by the chains from turning round their heads. Above and behind them a fire is blazing at a distance, and between the fire and the prisoners there is a raised way, like the screen which marionette players have in front of them, over which they show the puppets.

I see.

And do you see, I said, men passing along the wall carrying all sorts of vessels, and statues and figures of animals made of wood and stone and various materials, which appear over the wall? Some of them are talking, others silent.

You have shown me a strange image and they are strange prisoners.

Like ourselves, I replied; and they see only their own shadows, or the shadows of one another, which the fire throws on the opposite wall of the cave.

Plato, Republic

❦❦❦❦❦❦

And our Lord took me by the hand and made me enter a subterranean way where it is neither cold nor warm, where the sun does not shine and where rain and wind may not enter; a tunnel where I see nothing but a half-veiled glow from the downcast eyes in the face of my spouse . . . *I gladly consent to spend my entire life in this underground darkness to which he has led me; my only wish is that my gloom will bring light to sinners.* [Italics mine]

Saint Thérèse of Lisieux

❦❦❦❦❦❦

Who can map out the various forces at play in one soul? Man is a great depth, O Lord. The hairs of his head are easier by far to count than his feelings, the movements of his heart.

Saint Augustine

❦❦❦❦❦❦

This light puts the sensory and spiritual appetites to sleep, deadens them and deprives them of the ability to find pleasure in anything. It binds the imagination and impedes it from doing any good discursive work. It makes the memory cease, the intellect become dark and unable to understand anything, and hence it causes the will also to become arid and constrained, and all the faculties empty and useless. And over all this hangs a dense and burdensome cloud which afflicts the soul and keeps it withdrawn from God. As a result it [the soul] asserts that in darkness it walked securely.

Saint John of the Cross, *Dark Night of the Soul*

❧❧❧❧❧❧❧❧

'You are the master of cunning arts. I have a disease. Can you cure it, sir?'

'So far,' replied Wen Chih, 'you have only acquainted me with your desire. Please let me know first the symptoms of your disease.'

'I hold it no honour,' said Lung Shu, 'to be praised in my native village, nor do I consider it a disgrace to be decried in my native state. Gain excites in me no joy, and loss no sorrow. I look upon life in the same light as death, upon riches in the same light as poverty, upon my fellow men as so many swine, and upon myself as I look upon my fellow men. I dwell in my home as though it were a caravanserai and regard my native district with no more feeling than I would a barbarian state. Afflicted as I am in these various ways, honours and rewards fail to rouse me, pains and penalties to overawe me, good or bad fortune to influence me, joy or grief to move me. Thus I am incapable of serving my sovereign, of associating with my friends and kinsmen, of directing my wife and children, or of controlling my servants and retainers. What disease is this and what remedy is there that will cure it?'

Wen Chih replied by asking Lung Shu to stand with his back to the light, while he himself faced the light and looked at him intently. 'Ah!' said he after a while, 'I see that a good square inch of your heart is hollow. You are within an ace of being a true sage. Six of the orifices in your heart are open and clear, and only the seventh is blocked up. This however is doubtless due to the fact that you are mistaking for a disease that which is really divine enlightenment. It is a case in which my shallow art is of no avail.'

Musings of a Chinese Mystic

❧❧❧❧❧❧❧❧

Know the Self as lord of the chariot,
The body as the chariot indeed,
The discriminating intellect as
The charioteer, and the mind as the reins.
The senses, say the wise, are the horses;
Selfish desires are the roads they travel.
When the Self is confused, they point out,
With the body, senses, and mind, he seems
To enjoy pleasure and suffer sorrow.
When a man lacks discrimination and
His mind is undisciplined, his senses
Run hither and thither like wild horses.
But they obey the rein like trained horses

When he has discrimination and his
Mind is one-pointed. The man lacking
Discrimination, with little control
Over his thoughts, and far from pure, reaches
Not the pure state of immortality,
But wanders from death to death; while he who
Has discrimination, with a still mind
And pure heart, reaches journey's end, never
Again to fall into the jaws of death.
With a discriminating intellect
As charioteer, a disciplined mind as
Reins, he attains the supreme goal of life
To be united with the Lord of Love.

Katha Upanishad

"What is a butterfly?"

"It's what you are meant to become. It flies with beautiful wings and joins the earth to heaven. It drinks only nectar from the flowers and carries the seeds of love from one flower to another. Without butterflies the world would soon have few flowers."

"How can I believe there's a butterfly inside you or me when all I see is a fuzzy worm? How does one become a butterfly?"

"You must want to fly so much that you are willing to give up being a caterpillar."

"You mean to die?"

"Yes and no. What looks like you will die but what's really you will still live. Life is changed, not taken away. Isn't that different from those who die without every becoming butterflies?"

"If I decide to become a butterfly what do I do?"

"Watch me. I'm making a cocoon. It looks like I'm hiding, I know, but a cocoon is no escape. It's an in-between house where the change takes place. It's a big step since you can never return to caterpillar life. During the change it will seem to you or to anyone who might peek that nothing is happening—but the butterfly is already becoming. It just takes time! And there's something else. Once you are a butterfly, you can really love—the kind of love that makes new life. It's better than all the hugging caterpillars can do."

How could she risk the only life she knew when it seemed too unlikely she could ever be a glorious winged creature? What did she have to go on?—Seeing another caterpillar who believed enough to make his own cocoon; and that peculiar hope which leapt within her when she heard about butterflies.

"You'll be a beautiful butterfly—We're all waiting for you!"

She decided to risk being a butterfly. For courage she hung right beside the other cocoon and began to spin her own.

"Imagine, I didn't even know I could do this. That's some encouragement that I'm on the right track. If I have inside me the stuff to make cocoons—maybe the stuff of butterflies is there too."

A soul with an authentic desire for divine wisdom wants suffering first, in order to enter this wisdom by the thicket of the cross! Accordingly, Saint Paul admonished the Ephesians not to grow weak in their tribulations and to be strong and rooted in *charity* in order to comprehend with all the saints what is the breadth and height and depth, and to know also the supereminent charity of the knowledge of Christ, in order to be filled with all the fullness of God. The gate entering into these thickets of His wisdom is the cross which is narrow and few desire to enter by it, but many desire the delights obtained from entering here. [Italics mine]

Saint John of the Cross, *Dark Night of the Soul*

Just as the ultimate reason for everything is love (which is seated in the will), whose property is to give and not to receive, whereas the property of the intellect (which is the subject of essential glory) lies in receiving and not giving, the soul in the inebriation of love does not put first the glory she will receive from God, but rather puts first the surrender of herself to Him through true love, without concern for her own profit.

Saint John of the Cross

The deepest center of an object we take to signify the farthest point attainable by that object's being and power and force of operation and movement . . . . When once it [the object] arrives and has no longer any power or inclination toward further movement, we declare that it is in its deepest center.

The soul's center is God. When it has reached God with all the capacity of its being and the strength of its operation and inclination, it will have attained to its final and deepest center in God, it will know, love and enjoy God with all its might.

Saint John of the Cross, *The Living Flame of Love*

And thus, when the soul says that the flame wounds it in its deepest center, it means that it wounds it in the farthest point attained by its own substance and virtue and power.

Saint John of the Cross, *Living Flame of Love*

These effects are given by God when He brings the soul to Himself with the kiss sought by the bride . . . . Here an abundance of water is given to this deer that was wounded. Here one delights in God's tabernacle. Here the dove Noah sent out to see if the storm was over finds the olive branch as a sign of firm ground discovered amid the floods and tempests of this world.

Saint Teresa of Ávila

Ten Virgins

Then shall the kingdom of heaven be likened unto ten virgins, which took their lamps, and went forth to meet the bridegroom.

And five of them were wise, and five *were* foolish.

They that *were* foolish took their lamps, and took no oil with them:

But the wise took oil in their vessels with their lamps.

While the bridegroom tarried, they all slumbered and slept.

And at midnight there was a cry made, Behold, the bridegroom cometh; go ye out to meet him.

Then all those virgins arose, and trimmed their lamps.

And the foolish said unto the wise, Give us of your oil; for our lamps are gone out.

But the wise answered, saying, *Not so;* lest there be not enough for us and you: but go ye rather to them that sell, and buy for yourselves.

And while they went to buy, the bridegroom came; and they that were ready went in with him to the marriage: and the door was shut.

Afterward came also the other virgins, saying, Lord, Lord, open to us.

But he answered and said, Verily I say unto you, I know you not.

Watch therefore, for ye know neither the day nor the hour wherein the Son of man cometh.

The Gospel According to Saint Matthew

I am now speaking of that rain that comes down abundantly from heaven to soak and saturate the whole garden. If the Lord never ceased to send it whenever it was needed, the gardener would certainly have leisure; and if there were no winter but always a temperate climate, there would never be a shortage of fruit and flowers, and the gardener would clearly be delighted. But this is impossible while we live, for we must always be looking out for one water when another fails. The heavenly rain very often comes down when the gardener least expects it. Yet it is true that at the beginning it almost always comes after long mental prayer. Then, as one stage succeeds another, the Lord takes up this small bird and puts it into the nest where it may be quiet. He has watched it fluttering for a long time, trying with its understanding and its will and all its strength to find God and please Him; and now He is pleased to give it its reward in this life.

The Life of Saint Teresa

When I first knew Walt Whitman I used to think that he watched himself, and did not allow his tongue to give expression to feelings of fretfulness, antipathy, complaint and remonstrance . . . . After long observation . . . I satisfied myself that such absence or unconsciousness was entirely real. His deep, clear and earnest voice [contributed to] the charm of the simplest things he said . . . . He never spoke deprecatingly of any nationality or class of men, or time in the world's history . . . or against any trades or occupations—not even against any animals, insects, plants or inanimate things, nor any of the laws of nature, nor any of the results of the laws, such as illness, deformity or death. He never complained or grumbled either at the weather, pain, illness or anything else. He never in conversation . . . used language that could be considered indelicate . . . . He never spoke in anger . . . never exhibited fear, and I do not believe he ever felt it.

Richard Maurice Bucke, M.D.

When the soul is naughted and transformed, then of herself she neither works nor speaks nor wills, nor feels nor hears nor understands; neither has she of herself the feeling of outward or inward, where she may move. And in all things it is God who rules and guides her, without the mediation of any creature. And the state of this soul is then a feeling of such utter peace and tranquillity that it seems to her that her heart, and her bodily being, and all both within and without, is immersed in an ocean of utmost peace . . . . And she is so full of peace that though she press her flesh, her nerves, her bones, no other thing comes forth from them than peace.

Saint Catherine of Genoa

You sent me off to fetch one of Father's big glasses and had me put my little thimble by the side of it; then you filled them both up with water and asked me which I thought was the fuller. I had to admit that one was just as full as the other because neither of them would hold any more. That was the way you helped me to grasp how it was that in Heaven the least have no cause to envy the greatest.

Saint Thérèse of Lisieux, *Story of a Soul*

As a solid rock cannot be moved by the wind, the wise are not shaken by praise or blame. When they listen to the words of the dharma, their minds become calm and clear like the waters of a still lake.

Dhammapada

When a man's consciousness is unified, he leaves behind vain anxiety. He does not worry if actions proceed well or ill for him. Therefore, devote yourself to the disciplines of yoga, for yoga is skill in action.

Bhagavad Gita

To have peace in one's soul is the greatest happiness.

Oriental Wisdom

The knower and the known are one. Simple people imagine that they should see God, as if He stood there and they here. This is not so. God and I, we are one in knowledge.

Meister Eckhart

Whereas the enlightened man, by virtue of the divine light, is simple and stable and free from curious considerations, these others are manifold and restless and full of subtle reasonings and reflections; and they do not taste inward unity, nor the satisfaction which is without images. And by this they may know themselves.

John of Ruysbroeck

I see without eyes, and I hear without ears. I feel without feeling and taste without tasting. I know neither form nor measure; for without seeing I yet behold an operation so divine that the words I first used, perfection, purity, and the like, seem to me now mere lies in the presence of truth . . . . Nor can I any longer say, "My God, my all." Everything is mine, for all that is God's seem to be wholly mine. I am mute and lost in God.

Saint Catherine of Genoa

When your mind has overcome the confusion of duality, you will attain the state of holy indifference to things you hear and things you have heard.

When you are unmoved by the confusion of ideas, and your mind is completely united in love for the Lord of Love, you will attain the state of perfect yoga.

Bhagavad Gita

It is said that soon after his enlightenment, the Buddha passed a man on the road who was struck by the extraordinary radiance and peacefulness of his presence. The man stopped and asked, "My friend, what are you? Are you a celestial being or a god?"

"No," said the Buddha.

"Well, then, are you some kind of magician or wizard?"

Again the Buddha answered, "No."

"Are you a man?"

"No."

"Well, my friend, what then are you?"

The Buddha replied, "I am awake."

Buddhist

I no longer live within myself
And I cannot live without God
For if I have neither Him nor myself
What will life be?
It will be a thousand deaths,
Longing for my true life
And dying because I do not die.

Saint John of the Cross

Chapter III

Life at the Summit

. . . the butterfly can never rejoin the caterpillar as long as he lives. The butterfly is not an extraordinary caterpillar; rather, he is a different type altogether.

When the butterfly returns, the caterpillars do not recognize him anymore: he is an outsider. Nobody wants what he has to give; nobody is interested in his new knowledge. If the butterfly tries to give them some perspective on their creeping lives they are outraged, call him a fraud, and bring him down. They may even put him to death. Because the butterfly has returned full and overflowing, being dismissed, ignored, and misunderstood is a bewildering predicament. Like Santa Claus returning with good things for all men, he discovers he cannot give anything away. What we have here is no success story; there will be no glory in this unitive life. It will not be easy—Christ lasted only three years among the caterpillars. Yet to be put down, put out, and put away is the way it is supposed to go. To be rejected is the way forward now; it is the essence of the new movement, and what will demand the exercise of the full unitive life.

Bernadette Roberts

I CHOP WOOD!

When the Zen master attained enlightenment he wrote the following lines
to celebrate it:
"Oh wondrous marvel:
I chop wood!
I draw water from the well!"

🐦🐦🐦🐦🐦🐦

Without leaving his door
He knows everything under heaven.
Without looking out of his window
He knows all the ways of heaven.
The further one travels
The less one knows.
Therefore the sage arrives without going,
Sees all without looking,
Does nothing, achieves everything.

Tao Te Ching

🐦🐦🐦🐦🐦🐦

I reached in experience the Nirvana which is unborn, unrivaled, secure
from attachment, undecaying and unstained. This condition is indeed reached
by me which is deep, difficult to see, difficult to understand, tranquil, excellent,
beyond the reach of mere logic, subtle, and to be realized only by the wise.

Guatama Buddha

🐦🐦🐦🐦🐦🐦

The time of business does not with me differ from the time of prayer, and
in the noise and clatter of my kitchen, while several persons are at the same
time calling for different things, I possess God in as great tranquility as if I were
upon my knees at the blessed sacrament.

Brother Lawrence

🐦🐦🐦🐦🐦🐦

Suddenly is the soul oned to God when it is truly peaced in itself: for in
Him is found no wrath. And thus I saw when we are all in peace and in love,

we find no contrariness, nor no manner of letting through that contrariness which is now in us.

Julian of Norwich

❧❧❧❧❧❧❧❧

The contemplative life expands into activities which spring from this root and produce lovely and fragrant flowers. They spring from this tree of the love of God alone, for him alone, without anything of self-interest; and the fragrance of these flowers spreads all around, for the good of many. . . .

Saint Teresa of Ávila

❧❧❧❧❧❧❧❧

Whatever God does, the first outburst is always compassion.

Meister Eckhart

❧❧❧❧❧❧❧❧

On another occasion I was called upon to defend a frail eight year old girl against a large man who was about to beat her. The girl was terrified. It was my most difficult test. I was staying at a ranch and the family went into town. The little girl did not want to go with them, and they asked, since I was there, would I take care of the child? I was writing a letter by the window when I saw a car arrive. A man got out of the car. The girl saw him and ran and he followed, chasing her into a barn. I went immediately into the barn. The girl was cowering in terror in the corner. He was coming at her slowly and deliberately.

You know the power of thought. You're constantly creating through thought. And you attract to you whatever you fear. So I knew her danger because of her fear. (I fear nothing and expect good—so good comes!)

I put my body immediately between the man and the girl. I just stood and looked at this poor, psychologically sick man with loving compassion. He came close. He stopped! He looked at me for quite a while. He then turned and walked away and the girl was safe. There was not a word spoken.

Now, what was the alternative? Suppose I had been so foolish as to forget the law of love by hitting back and relying upon the jungle law of tooth and claw? Undoubtedly I would have been beaten—perhaps even to death and possibly the little girl as well! Never underestimate the power of God's love—it transforms! It reaches the spark of good in the other person and the other person is disarmed.

Peace Pilgrim

Love seeketh not itself to please,
Nor for itself hath any care,
But for another gives its ease,
And builds a Heaven in Hell's despair.

William Blake

I remember one experience when it said in the local newspaper I was going to speak at a church service. It showed my picture—front and back, wearing my lettered tunic. A man who belonged to that church was simply horrified to discover that this creature wearing a lettered tunic was about to speak at his church. He called his preacher about it, and he called his friends about it. Somebody told me who he was. I felt so sorry that I had somehow offended a man that I didn't even know. So, I called him!

"This is Peace Pilgrim calling," I said. I could hear him gasp. Afterward he told me that he thought I had called to bawl him out. I said, "I have called to apologize to you because evidently I must have done something to offend you, since without even knowing me you have been apprehensive about my speaking at your church. Therefore I feel I must somehow owe you an apology and I have called to apologize!"

Do you know that man was in tears before the conversation was over? And now we're friends—he corresponded with me afterward. Yes, the law of love works!

Peace Pilgrim

Love thyself last, cherish those hearts that hate thee.

Shakespeare

People will tell you that you do not need friends on this journey, that God is enough. But to be with God's friends is a good way to keep close to God in this life. You will always draw great benefit from them.

This is to love:
    bear with a fault and not be astonished,
    relieve others of their labor and take upon yourself tasks

to be done;
be cheerful when others have need of it;
be grateful for your strength when others have need of it;
show tenderness in love and sympathize with the weakness of others.
Friends of God love others far more, with a truer, more ardent and a more helpful love. They are always prepared to give much more readily than to receive even to their Creator.

Saint Teresa of Ávila

❧❧❧❧❧❧❧

Love thy neighbor as I have loved you.
Love your enemies, bless them that curse you; do good to them that hate you.

Jesus the Christ

❧❧❧❧❧❧❧

On the journey to Seville, the nuns stayed at a hermitage the first night and alternated between sleep on a cold, stone floor and praying. Day two: while a "depraved group of men drew knives and fought among themselves," the nuns stayed enclosed in their wagon to avoid a potentially nasty scene. Food was scarce, most days consisted of beans, bread, and cherries. The sisters felt fortunate if they could find "an egg for our Mother." Day three: the boatman cheated them. His boat would not hold all that he promised. A wagon broke loose and drifted downstream, nuns and provisions still aboard. While a few of the sisters fell to their knees crying out to God, the rest pulled on a rope, hoping to save them. They received a quick answer to their prayers—the wagon landed on a sandbank. Day four: Teresa [of Ávila] was so ill that they stopped for her to rest at an inn. The "room" in which she rested was previously used as a pig shed:

The little room was roofed like a shed and had no windows. If you opened the door the sun blazed in. The sun here is not like in Castille; it is much worse. They put me to bed, but I would have been better off on the floor for the bed was so uneven that I didn't know what way to lie; it was like a bed of sharp stones.

She neglected to mention the bugs, the swearing people, the dancing, and the tambourines.

Nancy D. Potts, *Women of Vision, Women of Peace*

❧❧❧❧❧❧❧

To love life and work is to be intimate with life's inmost secret.

Kahlil Gibran

ව**ව**වවවවවවවව

Power always protects the good of some at the expense of others. Only love can attain and preserve the good in all.

Thomas Merton

ව**ව**වවවවවවවව

The Path of Virtue

He who does not rouse himself when it is time to rise, who, though young and strong is full of sloth, whose will and thought are weak, that lazy and idle man never finds the way to knowledge.

What ought to be done is neglected, what ought not to be done is done; the desires of unruly, thoughtless people are always increasing.

But they whose whole watchfulness is always directed to their body, who do not follow what ought not to be done, and who steadfastly do what ought to be done, the desires of such watchful and wise people will come to an end.

He who says what is not goes to hell; he also who, having done a thing, says I have not done it. After death both are equal: they are men with evil deeds in the next world.

Better it would be to swallow a heated iron ball, like flaring fire, than that a bad unrestrained fellow should live on the charity of the land.

Four things does a reckless man gain who covets his neighbor's wife— demerit, an uncomfortable bed, thirdly, punishment, and lastly, hell.

As a grass blade, if badly grasped, cuts the arm, badly practiced asceticism leads to hell.

If anything is to be done, let a man do it, let him attack it vigorously! A careless pilgrim only scatters the dust of his passions more widely.

They who are ashamed of what they ought not to be ashamed of, and are not ashamed of what they ought to be ashamed of, such men, embracing false doctrines, enter the evil path.

They who fear when they ought not to fear, and fear not when they ought to fear, such men, embracing false doctrines, enter the evil path.

They who see sin where there is no sin, and see no sin where there is sin, such men, embracing false doctrines, enter the evil path.

They who see sin where there is sin, and no sin where there is no sin, such men, embracing the true doctrine, enter the good path.

A man does not become a Brahman by his plaited hair, by his family, or by birth; in whom there is truth and righteousness, he is blessed, he is a Brahman.

I do not call a man a Brahman because of his origin or of his mother. He is indeed arrogant, and he is wealthy; but the poor, who is free from all attachments, him I call indeed a Brahman.

Him I call indeed a Brahman who is free from anger, dutiful, virtuous, without appetites, who is subdued, and has received his last body.

Him I call indeed a Brahman who does not cling to sensual pleasures, like water on a lotus leaf, like a mustard seed on the point of a needle.

Him I call indeed a Brahman who without hurting any creatures, whether feeble or strong, does not kill nor cause slaughter.

Him I call indeed a Brahman who is tolerant with the intolerant, mild with the violent, and free from greed among the greedy.

Him I call indeed a Brahman from whom anger and hatred, pride and hypocrisy have dropped like a mustard seed from the point of a needle.

Him I call indeed a Brahman who utters true speech, instructive and free from harshness, so that he offend no one.

Him I call indeed a Brahman who takes nothing in the world that is not given him, be it long or short, small or large, good or bad.

Him I call indeed a Brahman who in this world has risen above both ties, good and evil, who is free from grief, from sin, and from impurity.

Dhammapada

When Ramana Maharshi lay dying, the cries of his devotees' grief reached his ears. He asked one of his attendants, "Why do they despair so deeply?" His attendant answered, "It is because you are leaving them, master." Ramana turned to his attendant in puzzlement, "But where do they think I could go?"

Hindu

Let us not be justices of the peace, but angels of peace.

Saint Thérèse of Lisieux

PERMISSIONS

Every reasonable effort has been made to determine authors and publishers and to obtain appropriate permission to reproduce the stories, parables, and sacred texts included in this volume. Grateful acknowledgment is made to the following publishers and authors for kindly granting permission to reprint material from their books.

"When Life Was Full There Was No History" and "The Empty Boat" from *Thomas Merton: The Way of Chuang Tzu*. Copyright © 1965 by The Abbey of Gethsemane. Reprinted by permission of New Directions Publishing Corp.

Excerpts from *The Book of Virtues*, edited by William J. Bennett. Copyright © 1993 by William J. Bennett. Used by permission of Simon & Schuster, publishers.

Excerpts from *The Notebooks of Paul Brunton*, Vols. 2,3 by Paul Brunton. Copyright © 1986 by Kenneth Thurston Hurst. Used by permission of Larson Publications, 4936 Route 414, Burdett, NY 14818, 607-546-9342.

Excerpts from *The Notebooks of Paul Brunton*, Vol. 5 by Paul Brunton. Copyright © 1987 by the Paul Brunton Philosophic Foundation. Used by permission of Larson Publications.

Excerpts from *The Collected Works of St. Teresa of Ávila*, Vol. 2 by St. Teresa of Ávila, translated by Kieran Kavanaugh, O.C.D. and Otilio Rodriguez, O.C.D. Copyright © 1980 by Washington Province of Discalced Carmelites, Inc. Used by permission of ICS Publications.

Excerpts from *Seeing the Invisible* by Meg Maxwell and Verena Tschudin (Arkana, 1990). Copyright © by Meg Maxwell and Verena Tschudin, 1990. Reproduced by permission of Penguin Books, Ltd., United Kingdom.

Excerpts from *The Philokalia*, Vols. 1,2,3, compiled by St. Nikodimos of the Holy Mountain and St. Makarios of Corinth. Translated and edited by G.E.H. Palmer, Phillip Sherrard, and Kallistor Ware. Copyright © 1981 by The Eling Trust.

"Crowfoot," "Indian Proverb," and "Seng-ts'-an 'Hsin-Hsin Ming' " from *The Earth Speaks* by Steve Van Matre and Bill Weiler. Published by The Institute for Earth Education.

Excerpts from *The Little Flowers of St. Francis*, copyright © 1985 by Professor E.M. Blaiklock and Professor A.C. Keys. Published by Servant Publications, Box 8617, Ann Arbor, Michigan 48107. Used with permission.

Excerpts from *Thomas Merton: The Wisdom of the Desert*. Copyright © 1960 by The Abbey of Gethsemane. Reprinted by permission of New Directions Publishing Corp.

"The Banyan Deer" from *The Hungry Tigress* by Rafe Martin. Reprinted by permission of Parallax Press.

Excerpts from *The Song of the Bird* by Anthony de Mello. Copyright © 1982 by Anthony de Mello, S.J. Used by permission of Doubleday, a division of Bantam Doubleday Dell Publishing Group, Inc.

Excerpts from *Taking Flight* by Anthony de Mello. Copyright © 1988 by Gujarat Sahitya Prakash. Used by permission of Doubleday, a division of Bantam Doubleday Dell Publishing Group, Inc.

"Rag Tag Army" from *The Way of the Wolf* by Martin Bell. Copyright © 1968, 1970 by Martin Bell. Published by Ballantine Books, New York. Used by permission of Martin Bell.

Excerpts from *Wisdomkeepers*. Copyright © 1990 by Harvey Arden and Steve Wall. Beyond Words Publishing, Inc., Hillsboro, Oregon, 1-800-284-9673.

Excerpts from *Peace Pilgrim: Her Life and Work in Her Own Words* compiled by Friends of Peace Pilgrim. Copyright © 1982 by Friends of Peace Pilgrim. Published by Ocean Tree Books. For a free copy of the book, write to The Peace Pilgrim Center, 43480 Cedar Ave., Hemet, CA 92344.

Excerpts reprinted from *The Bhagavad Gita* and *The Dhammapada*, translated by Eknath Easwaran. Copyright © 1985, by permission from Nilgiri Press, Tomales, CA 94971.

Excerpts from *Introduction to the Devout Life* by St. Francis de Sales, translated by John K. Ryan. Used by permission of Doubleday.

Reprinted by permission of The Putnam Publishing Group/Jeremy P. Tarcher, Inc. from *What We May Be* by Piero Ferrucci. Copyright © 1982 by Piero Ferruci.

Excerpts from *Meister Eckhart: A Modern Translation* by Raymond Bernard Blakney. Copyright © 1941 by Harper & Brothers; copyright renewed.

Excerpts from *The Sacred Pipe: Black Elk's Account of the Seven Rites of the Oglala Sioux*, edited by Joseph Epes Brown. Published by University of Oklahoma Press.

"Who Am I?" from *Letters and Papers from Prison*, revised edition, by Dietrich Bonhoeffer. Copyright © 1953. Used by permission of The Macmillan Company, publisher.

Excerpts from *Tales of a Magic Monastery*. Copyright © 1981 by Cistercian Abbey of Spencer, Inc. Reprinted by permission of The CROSSROAD Publishing Company, New York.

Excerpts from *The Teachings of the Essenes From Enoch to the Dead Sea Scrolls*, by Edmond Bordeaux Szekely. Used by permission of I.B.S. Internacional.

Excerpts from *The Essene Teachings of Zarathustra* by Edmond Bordeaux Szekely. Used by permission of I.B.S. Internacional.

Excerpts from *As The Flower Sheds its Fragrance* by Anandamayi Ma. Copyright © 1983 by Shree Anandamayee, Charitable Society, Calcutta.

Excerpts from *The Way of the Sufi* by Idries Shah. Copyright © 1968 by Idries Shah. Used by permission of Dutton Signet, a division of Penguin Books USA, Inc.

Excerpts from *The Secret Path* by Paul Brunton. Copyright © 1935, 1963 by Kenneth Thurston Hurst. Used by permission of Samuel Weiser, Inc.

Excerpts from *Think on These Things* by Jidder Krishnamurti, edited by D. Rajagopal. Copyright © by D. Rajagopal. Used by permission of HarperCollins Publishers, Inc.

Excerpts from *The Collected Works of St. John of the Cross*, translated by Kieran Kavanaugh, O.C.D. and Otilio Rodriguez, O.C.D. Copyright © 1979 by Washington Province of Discalced Carmelites, Inc. Published by Institute of Carmelite Studies.

Excerpts from *Tales of the Hassidim* by Martin Buber. Copyright © 1947, 1948 by Schocken Books, Inc. Reprinted by permission of Schocken, published by Pantheon Books, a division of Random House, Inc.

"To a Beggar with a Mite" from *Stories of Mother Teresa* by José Luis González-Balado, translated by Olimpia Diaz. Copyright © 1983 by Liguori Publications. Used by permission of Liguori Publications.

Excerpts from *A Promise of Light* by Rodney R. Romney. Copyright © 1978 by Rodney R. Romney. Used by permission of Judson Press.

Excerpts from *Autobiography of a Yogi*. Copyright © 1946, renewed 1974 by Self-Realization Fellowship. Published by Self-Realization Fellowship, Los Angeles, CA. Reprinted by permission.

Excerpts from *New English Bible*. Copyright © Oxford Press and Cambridge University Press, 1961, 1970.

Excerpts from *The Holy Bible* authorized King James Version. Published by World Bible Publishers, Inc.

Excerpts from *The Varieties of Religious Experience* by William James. Published by Doubleday.

Excerpts from *Touching Peace* by Thich Nhat Hanh. Copyright © 1992 by Thich Nhat Hanh. Used by permission of Parallax Press.

Excerpts from *The Spirituality of Imperfection* by Ernst Kurtz, Ph.D. and Katherine Ketcham. Copyright © 1992 by Ernst Kurtz, Ph.D. and Katherine Ketcham. Used by permission of Bantam Books, a division of Bantam Doubleday Dell Publishing Group, Inc.

Excerpts from *Meditations with Teresa of Ávila* by Camille Campbell. Used by permission of Bear & Co., Inc.